BEYOND SUCCESS

IIII

REDEFINING
THE MEANING OF
PROSPERITY

JEFFREY L. GITTERMAN

AMACOM
AMERICAN MANAGEMENT ASSOCIATION
NEW YORK · ATLANTA · BRUSSELS · CHICAGO · MEXICO CITY · SAN FRANCISCO
SHANGHAI · TOKYO · TORONTO · WASHINGTON, D.C.

3 1257 01811 0667

Special discounts on bulk quantities of AMACOM books are available to corporations, professional associations, and other organizations. For details, contact Special Sales Department, AMACOM, a division of American Management Association, 1601 Broadway, New York, NY 10019.
Tel: 212-903-8316   Fax: 212-903-8083   E-mail: specialsls@amanet.org
Website: www.amacombooks.org/go/specialsales
To view all AMACOM titles go to: www.amacombooks.org

This publication is designed to provide accurate and authoritative information in regard to the subject matter covered. It is sold with the understanding that the publisher is not engaged in rendering legal, accounting, or other professional service. If legal advice or other expert assistance is required, the services of a competent professional person should be sought.

Library of Congress Cataloging-in-Publication Data

Gitterman, Jeffrey L.
  Beyond success : redefining the meaning of prosperity / Jeffrey L. Gitterman.
      p.   cm.
  Includes index.
  ISBN-13: 978-0-8144-1336-4
  ISBN-10: 0-8144-1336-6
  1. Spiritual life. 2. Personal coaching. 3. Success. I. Title.

  BL624.G554   2009
  178—dc22

                                          2008048313

Printing number
10 9 8 7 6 5 4 3 2 1

LESLIE,
THANK YOU FOR HELPING ME
REACH MY HIGHEST POTENTIAL, AND
FOR NOT BEING AFRAID TO PUSH ME
WHEN I NEEDED IT THE MOST.
JEFF

CONTENTS

ACKNOWLEDGMENTS

I AM MOST GRATEFUL TO MY FAMILY—LESLIE, JUSTIN, JAKE, JOELLE, and Gianna—for filling my life with love, light, and laughter. To Ellen Daly, whose inspiration in helping me find the right words to convey my message reached beyond all my expectations. To my wonderful literary agent Cynthia Zigmund and to all the people at AMA for believing in me. To Andrew Appel for his tireless efforts to put out the best book we possibly could. And to my family at Gitterman & Associates for their constant loyalty and support in making my visions a reality.

BEYOND
SUCCESS

INTRODUCTION

I'm talking to everyone
. . . but you're the one listening

BACK IN THE LATE NINETIES, I WAS INVITED BY A FRIEND TO see the Blue Man Group perform in New York City. I'd heard great things about their shows, so I was excited at the opportunity to see them myself. We took our seats and waited for the show to begin. As the lights dimmed, the packed theater slowly fell silent, but nothing happened on the stage. People around me began talking and rustling popcorn bags. Then, all of a sudden, my friend asked me to switch seats with him. And to my surprise, I heard a quiet but distinct voice that seemed to be coming out of a plastic tube attached to the armrest of my seat, addressing me by name.

"Jeff! Jeff! I need your help."

"What do you mean?" I asked

"Your friend who was sitting there before said you're the guy who can help me. I need you to start the show!"

Taken aback, I looked more closely and saw that the tube went right down through the floor. That was where the voice came from, the voice that was now calmly explaining to me that every Blue Man Group show starts with a member of the audience leading the entire audience in the "Blue Man Group War Whoop," which I was then shown how to do.

All I could think was that this was some joke, that I was being set up to be humiliated in front of a fairly large audience. My heart raced and my palms started to sweat. Convinced I would end up looking like an idiot, I leaned down into the tube and said, "You're out of your mind! And why are you talking to me, anyway?" And to this day, the reply I got was something I've never forgotten: *"I'm talking to everybody, but you're the one listening."*

Okay, I thought, so I got up out of my seat and yelled to everyone to follow me. Out of the few hundred people in the two-tier theater, perhaps twenty or so joined me in the war whoop. Embarrassed, I quickly sat back down.

The voice from the tube said, "Dude, that was lame."

So I got up again and screamed and hollered and jumped up and down until everyone in the theater joined in. Literally, every person in each tier of the theater stood up as I demanded that they follow me or else I would not start the show for them. When I took my seat again, the voice said, "You da man."

At the time, this event didn't mean much more to me than any other uncomfortable situation. But some years later, I had a vivid flashback to that moment in the theater, and the words and events took on a whole new meaning for me. I realized that I had learned two very important things from that strange encounter:

1. The most important voice that is speaking to us is usually the one asking us to do something that takes courage, something that takes us out of our comfort zone. That's why we so often ignore that voice and listen only to the endless chatter of our minds.

2. When we do listen to that voice and find the courage to step out of our comfort zone, we discover that one person can have an extraordinary impact.

Over time, this incident has become my metaphor for life, and it informs all of the principles that I'll be sharing in this book.

These principles are simple, but I firmly believe that if enough people adopted them, it could make a real difference in the world. But changing the world starts with changing individuals. So I ask you to read this book not as an observer or a philosopher but as a change agent. The lessons I have learned over the past few years have allowed me to be more present in every aspect of life and to live my life more fully. I've also come to realize that everyone has this capability within. That voice that I heard is within everyone—we just have to learn how to listen.

CHAPTER ONE

REDEFINING SUCCESS

I dread success.
—*GEORGE BERNARD SHAW*

MOST CLASSIC "SUCCESS STORIES" GO SOMETHING LIKE this:

I had nothing, then I discovered a new way of thinking, turned my life around and got everything I ever wanted. . . .

I could tell you one such story. I could probably even make it fill a whole book. I really did go from debt and depression to everything I'd ever wanted—in the space of just two years. It all started back in 1997, when I was just another New Jersey insurance salesman, trying to support a wife and two kids on less than $20,000 a year, falling months behind with the mortgage payments, scared and unsure of my future. Every evening when I got home from work, I would hide my car in a different part of the neighborhood because the finance company told me they were coming to repossess it. The debt collectors were calling every day, and my wife at the time was close to a nervous breakdown. I had credit card debt, mortgage debt, car loans. Things looked pretty bleak. And then one day, thanks to a life-changing conversation, I changed

1

my way of thinking. And within only two years—but wait a minute. That's actually not what this book is about.

Yes, I turned it all around. I started my own company, rose to the top of my profession, and increased my income to twenty times what I had been making. I got the money, the house, the car—the life of my dreams. And in this book, I will share with you some of the steps I took to get there. But before I do that, I want to jump ahead to the most important part of my story, which began once I'd got everything I ever wanted. Because what I discovered was that success was not what I thought it was. To put it very simply, I got everything I had ever wanted but found that I still wasn't happy. There was still something missing. I couldn't quantify it, but I just didn't feel the way I thought I should feel.

I remember when it began to dawn on me. It was the year my youngest son was diagnosed with autism. That wasn't the source of my unhappiness, but as anyone who has dealt with a life-changing event like this will know, it makes you reflect on what really matters. When I took an honest look at my own life, I realized that I was successful, in all the ways I had longed to be, but deeply, I didn't feel fulfilled.

▋▋▋▋

What I discovered was that success was not what I thought it was.

▋▋▋▋

The word *fulfilled* can mean a lot of different things to different people. The best way I can describe what it meant to me is that I thought I would reach a place where I could rest. I thought that once I had everything I wanted, I would reach a state of peace and contentment. I wasn't looking to retire, but I thought that internally I would feel at rest. For my whole life I had been struggling to get something, and I thought that once I got it all—once I crossed the finish line, reached the pot of gold—that struggle would be over.

And I really did get the pot of gold. It wasn't just everything I had ever wanted; it was more than I could even have imagined wanting. I had grown up in a tiny apartment in Queens, New York, sharing a bedroom with my sister. My father never made more than $35,000 a year. My substantial six-figure income was more money than that kid could ever have conceived of. And I just kept buying more stuff and going on more vacations and spending more money, and it never felt like there was enough money, because I still felt that I was chasing something. I wanted to feel at peace with myself. I had "everything," but this insistent voice inside me kept saying, "This isn't it." I didn't know what else there was. I didn't know where I was going anymore. And slowly it dawned on me that no matter how much money I made it would never make me feel the way I wanted to feel.

Of course, I wasn't the first person to discover that money does not necessarily equal happiness. These days there are countless books, articles, and global research projects dedicated to the topic. The so-called "science of happiness" will not only tell you that money won't make you happy, but it will give you cultural, psychological, physical, economic, and evolutionary explanations as to why. In his book *The Mind of the Market,* economist Michael Shermer makes a persuasive if rather uninspiring case that happiness or satisfaction is an entirely relative emotion, a combination of genetic predisposition and how well we measure up in comparison to our neighbors. "Because our sense of happiness tends to be based on . . . what others have, the pursuit of some absolute value that we believe will finally bring us happiness once we have achieved it paradoxically leads to misery when the goalposts keep moving,"[1] he writes. Daniel Gilbert, in the best-selling *Stumbling on Happiness,* draws on neuroscience, psychology, philosophy, and economics to weave an elaborate explanation of why we are so often unsatisfied even when we get the things we thought we wanted. "We treat our future selves as though they were our children," he says, "spending most of the hours of most of our days constructing tomorrows that we hope will make them happy . . . squirreling away portions of our paychecks each month so that *they* can enjoy their retirements on a putting green, jogging and flossing with some regularity so that *they* can avoid coronaries and gum grafts."[2] In this witty and entertaining yet rather disheartening tone, he paints a picture of most of us as well-intentioned but naive, performing daily "acts of charity" for our future selves who, "like the fruits of our loins . . . are often thankless."[3]

While all this analysis is fascinating and helps to make sense of why we are the way we are, I wonder if it is really helping people to change—or to be happier. It may be a truism that money doesn't buy happiness (although Gertrude Stein insists that was said by someone who didn't know where to shop), but when I look around at the consumer frenzy of our culture, I can't help but feel that we haven't got the message yet. Decades of happiness research don't seem to have amounted to a slowing down of what economists call the *hedonic treadmill,* the seemingly insatiable pursuit of material things we think will bring us satisfaction.

A treadmill is a good analogy. I've also heard it described it as a hamster wheel, or an eddy at the side of a stream. What these images point to is that we seem to be stuck in a closed loop when it comes to the pursuit of success, happiness, or fulfillment. And knowing that the loop doesn't work is not necessarily helping us get out of it. To break the loop, stop the treadmill, or get out of the hamster wheel, we need to look at not just the results of our efforts—"I still don't feel happy"—but at the underlying drives and convictions that make up the loop itself.

▌▌▌▌

To get out of the hamster wheel, we need to look beyond just the results of our efforts.

▌▌▌▌

If we keep doing the same thing over and over, even though it doesn't produce the result we wanted, it must be because of certain unquestioned assumptions and motives that keep sweeping us back around into that stagnant eddy. Many of us live out our whole lives that way, because we haven't stopped to question these things.

The goal of this book is to help you create a meaningful definition of success, attain that success, and most important, actually be able to enjoy that success. To do that, let's start by taking a closer look at some of the fundamental issues. Let's talk about *money,* let's talk about *happiness,* let's talk about *desire,* and then let's talk about what success really means.

PUTTING MONEY BACK IN ITS PLACE

I'm a financial adviser, so money is a subject that's close to my heart. Often I like to open my seminars by asking people to give me definitions of what "money" means to them. I always get a similar range of replies: *freedom . . . security . . . opportunity . . . power.* I've asked this same question to hundreds of financial planners over the last several years, and I rarely hear the standard dictionary definition, which is simply that money is *a means of exchange.*

What's important about their answers is that they illustrate a general misunderstanding that many people have in relationship to money. The problem is not just that we think money can buy us things that will permanently make us happy, but also that we tend to define money itself in terms of states of being that we desire.

As Lynne Twist writes in *The Soul of Money*: "Money still facilitates the sharing and exchange of goods and services, but somewhere along the way the power we gave money outstripped its original utilitarian role. Now, rather than relating to money as a tool we created and control, we have come to relate to money as if it is a fact of nature, a force to be reckoned with. . . . Money only has the power that we assign to it and we have assigned it immense power."[4]

I define money as "a means to satisfy a desire." That sounds like a straightforward enough definition. Things get complicated, however, when we tend to *measure* our satisfaction, happiness, or success by how much money we have. In our culture, money is no longer simply a means but an end unto itself, trapping us in a closed loop.

As a financial planner, I see proof on a very regular basis that having a million dollars in the bank has no relationship to happiness—but people continue to insist that it does, even though their own experience contradicts this idea. Many of my clients who have reached that milestone tell me that they still wake up in the morning and feel like they did when they were broke. I've observed an interesting phenomenon among these clients. If their net worth is hovering just around the million-dollar mark, the markets, being what they are, tend to play games with them. They look at the numbers and see that one day they have just over $1 million, and the next day, it has dipped back into six figures. In reality, these fluctuations have absolutely no impact on their daily existence. And yet many people freak out when they see the numbers dip. They are measuring their happiness by a financial marker to such a degree that these fluctuations begin to control their day-to-day emotional states.

In our culture, money is no longer simply a means but an end unto itself.

Back in the nineteenth century, the philosopher Arthur Schopenhauer wrote, "Money is human happiness in the abstract; and so the man who is no longer capable of enjoying such happiness in the concrete, sets his whole heart on money."[5] I love that quote because it is so true. In my work as a financial adviser, I meet far too many people who are living their lives in that "abstract" realm. They have concrete success (a spouse and two kids, a five-bedroom house plus a vacation home in the Caymans, a new BMW every two years, and they can actually pay for their children's college educations in cash), but they are unable to enjoy any of it. I have something of a unique vantage point in my work, because my client base includes 3,500 college professors—men and women with not only an unusual degree of financial stability but also more job security and free time than most. And yet even among this demographic, I see degrees of happiness and fulfillment that vary extraordinarily.

I'm not arguing against the importance of money—as Woody Allen put it in his inimitable manner, it's "better than poverty, if only for financial reasons."[6] That's a funny quote, but it makes a very important point: It puts money in its place. Money itself is a neutral force—it is not good or evil, moral or immoral. Some Christians love to quote the Bible as telling us that "money is the root of all evil," but I think it would be more accurate to say that "*attachment to money* is the root of all evil." That makes a lot more sense. After all, money is currency, and the word *currency* comes from the Latin "currentum," which means "a condition of flowing." If money gets clogged up with meanings and desires that we have assigned to it, whether it is blocked out of our lives or hoarded in our bank accounts, then it is little wonder it becomes unhealthy, like a stagnant pool cut off from the current of a river.

FORGETTING ABOUT HAPPINESS

Implicit in the statement "money won't buy you happiness" is the idea that something else will, even though we don't quite know what that something is. Most of us are searching for that elusive something, whether it is through money, love, work, spiritual pursuits, or (if things get too difficult) alcohol or drugs. Look at your own life for a moment and see if finding this "thing" that will make you happy is what drives you. It is quite possible that you even bought this book for that very reason. But I'd better warn you right now that I don't have the key to perfect happiness. Why? Because I don't think that's the goal anyway.

What do we mean when we say "happiness"? Usually it represents a certain emotional state—a feeling of peace, joy, contentment, satisfaction—that we may have experienced in brief moments of our lives and that we want to experience permanently. But I think that's a myth—a fairy tale that has us all running in circles trying to reach a goal that is unreachable. That's what I spent the first few decades of my life doing, until I discovered that not only would money not buy me that feeling, but short of perhaps leaving the world behind and retiring to a cave in the Himalayas, there wasn't much chance of me getting it any time soon.

▌▌▌▌

Even surrounded by everything you could ever need, you could still experience emotional states that you have no control over.

▌▌▌▌

Just think about how hard it is to sustain any particular state of being for more than a few minutes or a few hours at most. Next time you feel happy, try it—see how long you can hold onto that feeling before something triggers a negative emotion and happiness slips out of your grasp. That's just how human beings are.

Our emotional experience fluctuates constantly, based on any number of factors: internal and external, rational and irrational, objective and subjective, biological, psychological, environmental, chemical . . . the list could go on and on. If you stop and think for a moment about the confluence of circumstances, inner and outer, that you would have to achieve in order to control all these factors on a permanent basis, you'll quickly see that this level of control is impossible.

Even if you isolated yourself in a beautiful place, surrounded by everything you could ever need, and meditated all your waking hours, your hormones could still trigger emotional states that you have no control over. And you'd probably get lonely. The point is, our emotional experience is not something we can completely control. And yet most people in our culture unquestioningly believe that the ultimate goal is to be "happy" 24/7. If that's how we define success, we are probably setting ourselves up for failure.

DESIRE AND THE BRAIN

It is our very definition of happiness that gets us caught in a closed loop of always wanting more of what we can't seem to get. We set this bar called "happiness," and we have some idea of something we *want* that will make us happy. When we imagine getting that thing—whether it is a lover or a house with an ocean view or a better job—we feel a sense of exhilaration. American spiritual teacher Andrew Cohen calls this "the promise of perfection" that is created through the power of our own desire. He writes, "It's very extraordinary when we discover that the most exciting part of the whole process is the wanting itself. . . . To the ego and personality, happiness is equated with the thrill of wanting to possess, wanting to acquire."[7] The problem is that as we all know, when we get the things we want, they usually don't live up to our expectations.

I remember saving my allowance for months and months to buy my first bike. I would walk past that store window every day on my way home from school and gaze at it—the shiny spokes, the flawless red paint. It was magnetic. And I can still taste the thrill of the day I finally walked into that shop, emptied out my savings, and wheeled that bike out into the street—and the curious sense of deflation or let down that seemed to have slowly descended on me out of nowhere by the time I woke up the next morning. It was a great bike and I had a lot of fun with it. But that special something—that magic—had gone. Cohen uses the examples of a new car and a new lover, and comments: "It's revealing to see that, from a certain point of view, the experience with the car and the experience with the [person] we long to possess are not that different." This is because "We are not seeing the car as it truly is; we are not seeing the one we long to possess as he or she truly is. What we are seeing is our own imagination fueled by the weight of our desire."

||||

The loop continues because when we feel that sense of let-down, we immediately start looking for the next thing that we imagine will make us happy. We raise the bar, setting our sights on a newer, younger, more beautiful, or bigger, better, faster object of desire. And we feel that sense of anticipation again, which convinces us that "this is it."

Scientists these days can even explain the physiology of why this happens. It has to do with the way our brains are wired. Financial writer Jason Zweig, in his entertaining and insightful book *Your Money and Your Brain,* describes going to a neuroscience lab at Stanford to participate in an experiment on this matter. He was put inside a scanner that traced his brain activity while he played an investing video game. What the study showed was that in those moments when Zweig *anticipated* a big win, the neurons in a certain part of the brain went wild. By contrast, whenever he actually won some money, the response measured by the scanner was far less intense. What this experiment revealed, tested on Zweig and many others, is that the human brain is wired to experience more pleasure in the *anticipation* of a reward than in getting the actual reward. Modern science was able to prove, as Danish philosopher Søren Kierkegaard observed almost two centuries earlier, that "the fulfillment is always in the wish."[8]

I see this all the time in my kids. They use up so much energy in *wanting* whatever the latest thing is—a puppy, a new cell phone, a pair of designer sneakers, a video game—but when they get it, they suddenly don't seem so interested, and before I know it, they are wanting the next thing.

I won't try to explain the complex physiology of what scientists call the "seeking system" here, although I would recommend *Your Money and Your Brain* for anyone interested. But the point that is relevant, and has been backed up by numerous studies, is that, as Zweig puts it, "The pleasure you *expect* tends to be more intense than the pleasure you *experience*."[9] There are evolutionary reasons for this phenomenon, and it no doubt has played an essential role in keeping our species motivated to procreate and innovate our way to where we find ourselves today. But, as Zweig concludes:

> . . . [T]he seeking system in our own brains functions partly as a blessing and partly as a curse. Our anticipation circuitry forces us to pay close attention to the possibility of coming rewards, but it also leads us to expect that the future will feel better than it actually does once it arrives. That's why it's so hard for us to learn that the old saying is true: Money doesn't buy happiness. After all, it forever feels as if it *should*.[10]

BREAKING OUT OF THE LOOP

If nature designed us this way, how are we supposed to get out of the loop? Spiritual teachers since the time of the Buddha have offered answers to this question, ways to liberate the self from what contemporary Buddhists sometimes call the "wanting mind." The Buddha believed that *tanha,* the blind craving for objects or sensual pleasures, was the root of all suffering. Numbers two and three of the Four Noble Truths, which are the essence of Buddhism, state that "suffering arises from attachment to desires" and "suffering ceases when attachment to desire ceases."[11]

Buddhist teachings guide the spiritual aspirant to find liberation from *samsara,* which contemporary Tibetan Buddhist teacher Sakyong Mipham defines as "a wheel that is endlessly spinning . . . a circle of illusion that keeps us ending up just where we started."[12] Such schools of wisdom—be they Buddhist, Hindu, Taoist, or one of the many varieties of contemporary Western spirituality, such as the best-selling *Power of Now* by Eckhart Tolle—teach us to dwell in the present, rather than live in constant anticipation of the future. They can all show us powerful techniques for "living in the now" and enable us to taste moments of freedom from the endless craving of the mind. I highly recommend trying some of these practices, because they can actually short-circuit the endless loop of *samsara,* offering invaluable insight into the mechanisms of the mind.

> **‖‖**
>
> **Those of us who have not chosen a path of simplicity and seclusion need a solution to the desire loop that is more aligned with the reality of our lifestyles.**
>
> **‖‖**

The problem, however, with many of these approaches is that if we are not careful, those moments of "presence," freedom, and bliss simply become a new object of desire. We want to experience more freedom from wanting. Before we know it, we are back in the loop, chasing a temporary emotional experience in the hope of making it permanent. Trying to "live in the now" might work for a monk whose main employment is prayer, meditation, and service, and who lives a life of simplicity and seclusion. But for those of us who have not chosen that path, I feel we need a solution to the desire loop that is more aligned with the reality of our lifestyles, our environments, and our neurological programming. And we need it to be a solution that is completely integrated with our business and financial lives.

BEYOND SUCCESS

While success cannot be defined solely by the possession of external objects like houses, cars, and a new job title, neither can it be defined by the possession of internal states such as contentment and even happiness. To create a meaningful definition of success, I believe we need to find a different way to measure it, other than by outer wealth *or* inner feeling states.

When I got to that point in my own life where I found myself "successful" by common standards yet far from happy, I had to rethink what success was all about. I took a good honest look at my life. For the previous four years I had been chasing a dream, religiously visualizing my goals, and attaining them one by one. And I had found a lot of joy in that process. I didn't know then that my brain was wired this way, but I saw in my own experience that there was more joy in chasing the dream than in getting it. It wasn't so much that I was unhappy with the fruits of my success. There was nothing wrong with having the money, and it sure was nice not to have to worry about paying the bills each month. But I had attained everything and was missing that thrill that came from the pursuit itself.

Now, we could conclude from that experience, as many of the brain scientists do, that our evolutionary wiring is a kind of curse, condemning us to perpetual letdown. The anticipation mechanism can seem like a cruel trick of nature. But I looked at it another way. I realized that the problem wasn't that the goals I had reached weren't good enough. The problem was that I was standing still again. I had no journey anymore. And I understood that I needed a journey; I needed a direction; I needed a dream. So I started to turn my attention to the journey itself, to the sense of striving and reaching ever-higher, and decided to seek my happiness there, rather than in any particular outcome. I guess it's a kind of "living in the moment," but it is a moment that is always moving. This approach does not try to short-circuit the process of desire, but rather to channel that powerful motivational drive *outward.*

When we really understand that there is nothing we can *get* that will make us happy, we can stop striving to accumulate more and more. But because we are not made to stand still, we need to redirect our "seeking system," enlist it in the service of what we want to *express* in the world, rather than how we want to feel.

That's the key to this new approach—we have to become less concerned with how we happen to feel moment to moment. We have to stop judging our success by our emotional states. That seems like a simple enough thing to say, but it's not so easy to put into practice. The idea that success means a 24/7 "good feeling" is much more deeply ingrained in most of us than we realize. So the minute we start to feel dissatisfied, bored, depressed, anxious, or any of the countless not-so-positive things that we will almost inevitably feel for any number of reasons, most of which are beyond our control, we start concluding that "this isn't what I'm looking for" and we are back on the treadmill.

||||

When we really understand that there is nothing we can *get* that will make us happy, we can stop striving to accumulate more and more.

||||

14

The ironic thing is, we judge our own success by how we feel, but we don't apply the same standard to others. When we think about someone we admire greatly, who we would unequivocally say lived a successful life, does it matter to us how they *felt*? Do we even care about the inner experience of Martin Luther King, Nelson Mandela, or Mahatma Gandhi? We judge their success by the tremendous impact they had on the world. Do we think Mother Teresa was less successful in her mission because we now know, thanks to the publication of her journals, that she was plagued by doubt and desperation? Or do we simply look at how many lives she saved, and perhaps even feel a greater admiration knowing that she did it despite how she felt?

When we begin to pay less attention to our feeling states as a measure of our success, we will find that we have a tremendous resource of energy and attention at our disposal to begin to have an impact—on our own lives and on others around us. This is what I discovered when I set out to find what lies *beyond* success and to redefine success itself in the process. That's the story this book is about: my "beyond success story"—and hopefully yours, too.

I say "beyond success" because success, I have discovered, is not an end point, a state of outer wealth or inner peace that we can achieve and then stop. We human beings are not made to stop—we are creatures of change, curiosity, and creativity who need always to have our goals set a little *beyond* our reach. We thrive on challenge and engagement. "Happiness," as Franklin D. Roosevelt said in his first inaugural address, "is not in the mere possession of money; it lies in the joy of achievement, in the thrill of creative effort."

I am convinced that this is what we are here for. We are de-

> **We are designed to give of *ourselves*—of our energy, our unique creative expressions, our talents, our strengths.**

signed to give of *ourselves*—of our energy, our unique creative expressions, our talents, our strengths. It is my deepest belief that we are each a unique vessel for the creative impulse that is animating life itself. And I feel that it is only through aligning our individual strengths with that universal source of creativity, in such a way that simultaneously fulfills our own deepest desires and serves others, that we will we find what could be called lasting happiness. Psychologist Mihaly Csikszentmihalyi (pronounced "chick-sent-me-high-ee") even sees this predicament as serving an evolutionary function. In his book *Good Business* he writes: "It is as if evolution has built a safety device in our nervous system that allows us to experience full happiness only when we are living at 100 percent—when we are fully using the physical and mental equipment we have been given."[13]

From an evolutionary perspective, this may just be a utilitarian safety device, but from an individual's perspective it is the key to completely turning your life around. It is the basis of the definition of success that's working for me every day, based on the lessons I've learned and the principles I've distilled from the last ten years—from my own continually evolving life story and the stories of many, many others I've had the pleasure of helping and learning from.

In the chapters that follow, I'll be exploring the essential principles of this definition, and then offering you Four Pillars on which to build your own *beyond success* story. It is my deepest conviction that this path can take you, as it took me, beyond everything you ever thought you wanted.

CHAPTER TWO

A NEW CURRENCY

*Tell me to what you pay attention and
I will tell you who you are.*

—*JOSE ORTEGA Y GASSET,*
Spanish philosopher and humanist (1883–1955)

THE MODEL OF SUCCESS THAT I WANT TO SHARE WITH YOU in this book does not use money as its primary currency. If we are to create a new model of success that is not measured by how much money we make or by how we feel moment-to-moment, we will need a new currency. Because money is merely representative and creates a lot of problems for us when used as the sole measure of our success, we need to begin by defining a new way of measuring and valuing our success.

As I mentioned earlier, the word *currency,* when translated from Latin, originally meant a "condition of flowing," and it was only given its common meaning of the "circulation of money" in 1699 by British philosopher John Locke. These terms we associate with money—flow and circulation—are very appropriate. Money is not something we can *create,* but we can encourage or block its flow into our lives. We can also encourage or block its flow out of our lives in ways that can be both healthy and unhealthy.

Traditionally, money has been assigned four characteristics, which old-fashioned economics textbooks had a rhyme for: "Money is a matter of functions four, a *medium, a measure, a standard, a store*." These days, the functions of money tend to be described as a *medium of exchange,* a *unit of account,* and a *store of value.*

I would add one more item to this list. It's a definition that you may not find in the economics books, but it is perhaps more relevant to true success than any of the standard definitions. And that is that money carries with it the flow of *energy.* Money, however tangible it may seem when we hold a fifty-dollar bill in our hand, is actually an abstract representation of something that seems intangible but has far more substance than pieces of paper. Energy is the lifeblood of capitalism.

When I say "energy," I don't just mean a physical feeling of being energetic as opposed to tired or lethargic. I mean the life force that human beings bring to whatever they engage with—be it a personal interaction or a creative collaboration, a physical challenge or a mental puzzle. When someone pays us for our work, what we are really giving them in return is our energy, directed toward the task of managing their business, selling their product, building a house, or performing whatever job we are hired for.

When I was a kid, I had an intuitive understanding, right or wrong, that everything in this world was really a movement of energy. I didn't buy the story that kept showing up in front of me, whether it was my parents' story or the story on the TV, that the world was made up of people, places, and things. I saw the world as energy.

▌▌▌▌

When someone pays us for our work, what we are really giving them in return is our energy . . .

▌▌▌▌

That understanding that I had naturally as a child is something that has for millennia been known to spiritual mystics, particularly in the Eastern traditions. Over the past thirty years, we have increasingly seen a greater synthesis of Eastern and Western thought than ever before, and many ancient teachings of the East have gained a wider acceptance in the West. And during that same time period, Western science has begun to validate some of the key insights of Eastern spirituality.

I love this quote from Max Planck, a German physicist and contemporary of Einstein who won a Nobel Prize for his research with atoms and is considered by many to be the father of quantum theory:

> As a man who has devoted his whole life to the most clear-headed science, to the study of matter, I can tell you as a result of my research about atoms this much: There is no matter as such. All matter originates and exists only by virtue of a force which brings the particle of an atom to vibration and holds this most minute solar system of the atom together. We must assume behind this force the existence of a conscious and intelligent mind. This mind is the matrix of all matter.[1]

Here is a scientist basically telling us that the fundamental element of reality is not matter, but energy. Quantum physicists today will tell you the same thing, usually in rather mind-twisting statements. But these ideas are not just the esoteric territory of the scientific fringe. Scientists have believed that the world can be completely understood in terms of energy for quite some time. In 1632, Galileo published *A Dialogue Concerning Two Chief World Systems,* which included his principle of relativity, which states that the fundamental laws of physics are universal in all fixed (i.e., stable and unalterable) situations.

Others, such as Isaac Newton and Albert Einstein, continued to build on the work of Galileo, which eventually led to the discovery of Einstein's famous theory of relativity in 1905. $E=mc^2$ states that energy equals mass times the speed of light squared, and that energy and mass are equivalent and transmutable.

More recently, scientists such as Stephen Hawking have been looking to take the work of Einstein further to find a complete set of laws on how everything in the universe works, in what has become known as Unified Field Theory. Although this theory has yet to be conclusively proven, it's hoped that in time it will be found and eventually simplified so that someday it can be taught in schools, thereby giving everyone some idea of how the universe operates.

Obviously that's a very brief summary of a much deeper and more complex subject, and there are certainly numerous books and other resources available detailing how physicists are trying to explain the nature of energy and matter in the universe, if anyone would like to understand it in more detail. But for our purposes, I hope we can simply agree that at the most basic level, energy is the value we are exchanging with each other and the world in every action and interaction.

Let's take some more practical examples. Most of us have heard that speech itself accounts for only a small percentage of the actual way in which we communicate. If this is so, what is the rest of that communication? Energy.

When I was a child, I used to find it hilarious that I could look at my dog and say in an angry tone of voice "You're a good dog!" and then watch his shoulders and tail slump as if he were being yelled at. Then I would turn around and say in a really loving voice, "You're a bad dog!" and I would crack up as he immediately straightened up and started wagging his tail as if he was being praised.

It is the same with human relationships. How often have you encountered someone who says one thing to you, but from the vibe you're picking up from that person, you know he means something quite different? Most people can probably say they've had the experience of putting a nice big smile on their face and saying "Hello" to someone they don't like, when all the while both people know they don't like each other. This probably happens in business more often than we'd like to admit. The "Hello" and the smile don't really change a thing, because it's not in the words. It's the energy behind the words.

Sometimes when I am speaking to businesspeople, they will agree with this basic premise—that energy is the basis of everything—but they complain that they find the concept of "energy" too vague or ungraspable. So I ask them, besides money, what is the currency through which we exchange our energy?

Here's a hint: It's something that we go to extraordinary lengths to get. Corporations and politicians spend billions of dollars for it, yet we will often give it away for free. Kids will misbehave to get some, and doctors even prescribe medication to control it. The answer, if you haven't already guessed, is *attention*.

WHERE ATTENTION GOES, ENERGY FLOWS

Attention may still seem too intangible to be considered a currency or a commodity. The dictionary defines attention as "concentration of the mind" or "a close or careful observing or listening." But these definitions do little to evoke the power of this intangible force—economic power, political power, social power, personal power. Think about the ways we use the word. We talk about *paying* attention. We *need* attention. Someone popular is *the center of attention*; someone needy is always trying to *get your attention*. As intangible as it may seem, attention is the currency of countless transactions we engage in every day.

Why is attention so powerful? Because what you choose to put your attention on is where you direct your *energy*—in all its many forms, including your time, your creativity, and of course, your money. Let's take a metaphor from the natural world. Our planet finds a basic source of energy in the molten ball of fire it is orbiting: the sun. Sunlight provides energy in the form of warmth, and plants have sophisticated systems to capture and convert that energy.

What human beings have discovered is that while sunlight in its natural form is a source of warmth, it doesn't have much power because it is spread out in so many directions. But when sunlight is focused and concentrated through a magnifying glass, it suddenly becomes far more powerful. When harnessed in this way, the power of sunlight can start a fire, providing warmth and energy that is much more intense. And when the power of light is condensed to a much greater degree, it becomes a laser that can cut through steel.

In the same way, your mind, with its power of attention, acts as a focusing agent for energy, a magnifying glass through which that energy can be amplified in its impact. If you really train your attention, it can become like a laser, a powerful tool for cutting through many of the illusions and misconceptions that keep most of us trapped in the kind of loop I described in the previous chapter—a loop of always wanting more of something we can't seem to get.

‖‖

As intangible as it may seem, attention is the currency of countless transactions we engage in every day.

‖‖

If you're still not convinced that attention is a commodity, let's look at how the major players in the corporate world relate to it. Attention may seem an intangible thing to label in this way, but its commercial power quickly becomes apparent when you look at the lengths others will go to get it. Corporations today spend thousands of dollars researching where their potential customers' attention goes as they surf the Web, and they spend thousands more creating sophisticated strategies to capture their customers' attention. It's no accident we talk about *"paying* attention."

If you've seen the 2002 movie *Minority Report,* you probably remember the scene where Tom Cruise's character walks into the mall, passes through a retina-scanning identification device, and is immediately besieged by personally tailored ads addressing him by name, anticipating his every desire. That seemed like a far-off sci-fi future when the movie came out, but these days something surprisingly similar happens every time you go online. Software now regularly tracks what sites you visit on the Internet, where you click, how long you stay on a page—in other words, what catches your attention—in order to present you with ads that match your interests.

Companies spend billions of dollars on marketing—advertising is the biggest expense for most companies—and the goal of it all is to catch your attention. So they pay other companies to figure out what you pay attention to. They want to know if you go online and look at a particular pair of designer jeans, a turbo-charged vacuum cleaner, a hybrid SUV, or a new ultra-slim phone. They even want to know which corner of the screen you look at first, and how many seconds you spend on each page.

Not only do companies try to catch your attention—they also sell it to other companies. Have you ever heard an ad-sales person trying to sell advertising space on a website? Salespeople don't say,

> **▌▌▌▌**
>
> **If you really train your attention, it can become a powerful tool for cutting through misconceptions that keep most of us trapped in a loop of wanting more of something we can't seem to get.**
>
> **▌▌▌▌**

"You should advertise on our site because we have the best web design or the most interesting content." They say, "You should advertise on our site because we have half a million visitors a week who spend an average of thirty seconds on our home page. And for just an additional $1,000, you can have our top right-hand corner, which is where 75 percent of our visitors click first." They are selling your attention, and the more of your attention they can claim to be capturing, the more money they can charge their advertisers. No wonder the Internet age has been dubbed an "attention economy."

"A wealth of information creates a poverty of attention," wrote pioneering economist Herbert Simon, in a remarkably prescient 1971 article.[2] With more and more corporations, politicians, entertainers, charities, and salesmen of all kinds competing for our attention, it's no wonder that we often feel as if our attention is scattered or fragmented.

Everywhere you look there is something vying for *your* attention. Observing this trend, media critic Thomas de Zengotita dubbed the contemporary self "the flattered self," pointing out that the "target of all representations—movies, documentaries, photographs, television, books, newspapers, messages, billboards, advertisements, brands, themed settings of all kinds—[is] you, the viewer, the reader, the consumer, the customer, the voter."[3]

Can you begin to appreciate why your attention is so valuable? I believe it is fast becoming one of the most valuable commodities of our time. And yet you are probably very far from being in control of this sought-after commodity. There are so many things vying for our attention that we have lost the ability to control where it goes. How often do you find yourself paying attention to some TV show when your wife or kids really need it more? You would never say that the TV was more important than your family, and yet it is quite likely that you unconsciously choose to "spend" your attention there rather than on those relationships that really matter to you. This kind of attention trade-off happens every day, but it's not something we are consciously in control of. Indeed, our attention can seem to have a mind of its own.

Our information-saturated lifestyles are only making this situation worse. Recent studies show that those of us who have grown up watching television have actually been unconsciously trained to track rapid movements of information—that's why we find watching TV numbing and soothing. Our kids need even more stimulus and can watch TV, send instant messages, and play a video game all while listening to their iPod. These days, our TV screens often carry one, two or three additional messages in the space around the picture we're watching, and when it comes to the Internet, there can be countless attention-grabbers on a single page, not to mention the pop-ups. When you think about it, all this clamoring for our attention seems like it would be exhausting, but have you ever noticed that it's a lot easier to watch television than it is to do something like meditate? That's because our attention is so accustomed to being drawn outward, pulled here and there by a multitude of competing objects.

You would never say that the TV was more important than your family, yet you probably choose to "spend" your attention there rather than on relationships that really matter to you.

According to the National Institute of Mental Health, between 3 percent and 5 percent of children (approximately 2 million in the United States) suffer from Attention Deficit Hyperactivity Disorder (ADHD). One company called Play Attention has developed specialized video games designed to help children learn to focus—and demonstrate the extraordinary power of attention in the process. Picture a computer screen with an image of a scuba diver floating on the top of an ocean. The child puts on a helmet with electrodes that pick up signals from the brain and send the information to the computer. Without touching a mouse or a keyboard, the child focuses her attention on the scuba diver, "willing" him to dive to the bottom of the ocean. And he does. But if the child's attention wanders, or the child is distracted by something happening in the room, the scuba diver bobs back to the surface. Now imagine trying to play that game while you walk down the street in New York City, and you'll see why most of us have so little control over our attention.

Back in the fifties, there was an outcry when market researcher James McDonald Vicary came up with the concept of "subliminal advertising" and declared that he was sending moviegoers hidden messages telling them to "eat popcorn" and "drink Coca-Cola." The whole thing was later found to be a hoax, but it hit a nerve. We feel vulnerable to things like subliminal advertising and brainwashing because we know we're not really in control of our attention. And corporations know it, too. That's why they are willing to invest so much money in trying to figure out ways to capture your attention for their products, causes, or services.

I hope I've convinced you by now that attention is a commodity—a source of value that you are being solicited for constantly, a currency that you are already conducting business in every day, whether or not you are conscious and in control of it. And these transactions are not just business-related. Attention is also the currency of our most personal relationships, and it is often in these areas that we find ourselves the most impoverished.

Let's take an example: Have you ever gotten to the end of the day feeling overwhelmed, out of control, and exhausted, even though you've barely left your desk? At times like that, have you felt that you don't have the energy to go home to your family and to the demands of your kids? In those moments, don't you just long for someone to listen to you? For most of the busy professionals that I work with, the scenario I have described is all too common. What people have often not considered, however, is that the experience of being overwhelmed is not just a result of the multitude of external pressures they are dealing with every day. It is often a result of the fact that we have lost control of our own attention. And since our attention controls how we spend our energy, the less control we have over it, the more "spent" we become.

‖‖‖

Attention is the currency of our most personal relationships . . .

‖‖‖

These days, whether in the workplace or simply walking down a city street, we are bombarded with competing demands for our attention; we are pulled this way and that by e-mail, phone calls, billboards, window displays, and people knocking at our doors.

Even I am asking for your attention as you read this book. You've made the time to sit and read because you think it is worthy of your attention. But then your cell phone rings, and you see it's your buddy from work. Or perhaps your neighbor and his wife are having an argument in the backyard. Or maybe you see a pile of bills sitting on the table that need paying. In any of these and countless other scenarios that happen every day, you are likely to momentarily forget about the book as your attention skips to wondering if your buddy got tickets to the game tonight, or thinking it's about time your neighbor left that foul-mouthed husband of hers, or worrying about where the money will come from this month.

You may choose to come back to reading the book, or any other activity you may be engaged in that you have decided is significant and valuable, but your flow of attention has been broken, and it will take you some time to reconnect to where you were.

Zoltan Torey, a blind man who has devoted his life to studying consciousness, has said that the average person's attention skips around every five seconds. And he should know. Torey's story is one of the most extraordinary testimonies to the power of attention that I have ever heard. An Australian psychologist and consciousness researcher, Torey lost his sight in a factory accident in 1951. Permanently blinded by acid at the age of twenty-one, he turned around at the brink of death and taught himself to "see without eyes" by training his visual imagination to an unprecedented degree. He explains that,

> My thoughts were now being projected onto this internal gray canvas in my mind, almost like in a movie theater. I began to watch and experience this mental imagery in an ever more intensive way . . . I just began to try to picture what was out there. . . . [M]y continuous efforts to visualize my surroundings did begin to generate in me an imaginary world, a world which became increasingly intense, accurate, and sharp."

Through training his attention in this way, Torey generated what he describes as a state of "intensive, vivid, daytime dreaming [in which] I had volition, and I could smell, hear, and touch, and that anchored the visual imagery into a concrete, tangible reality for me." After a year or two, he says, "This became such a powerful and effective process that . . . I was living continuously in a visual reality."

His "new sense" enables him to live a life unlike any blind person has ever lived before, whether he is going sightseeing, enjoying tennis on television, teaching himself how to use a typewriter, or even climbing up on his rooftop by himself (to his neighbors' amazement and alarm) and replacing all the gutters. It has carried him through honors degrees in psychology and philosophy, brought him success as a professional psychologist, and ultimately made it possible for him to tackle one of the most intractable problems known to science and philosophy alike—the riddle of the nature and origins of consciousness.

Rather than allowing himself to feel victimized by his disability, Torey was able turn it into a unique opportunity. He explains, "I saw in this a very clear-cut agenda for me to follow. I thought to myself, 'What if I could contribute to the trend of evolution by helping to shed light on the nature of consciousness itself?'" This sense of a personal mission and greater purpose is what has fueled his extraordinary achievements, but the foundation of all of it is the tremendous effort he made to "constantly direct and redirect [his] attention to problems that otherwise would not yield."[4]

When it comes to understanding the power of attention, one of my greatest teachers is my autistic son. He demands so much emotional and mental attention that I have very little left for myself. When he was young, I would try to defend myself from his constant draining of my energy in any way possible. I would work longer hours in order to be away. As I matured, I gradually learned that when I was with him, I had to drop the need to put my attention anywhere else so that I could focus solely on him. And these were the moments when my son was most content, as his repetitive behaviors would subside and his overall state of being would go from anxiety to calm. I began to see that if I could give him the attention he was looking for, he would often crawl into my lap and finally relax. I soon began to realize that this is true of everyone: When the light of attention is shone on another, their constant need and desire for "more" can be soothed, because ultimately it is just attention that we want anyway.

If you have children of your own, or have spent much time with the children of friends, you probably know that kids crave attention. In fact, many kids want attention much more than they care whether it is positive or negative. If children discover that the only way to get attention from their parents is to misbehave, they will go ahead and misbehave, even though the desired attention will likely come in the form of a punishment. The need for attention will outweigh the fear of the punishment that comes with it.

Our desire for attention is not a negative thing based on neediness.

Another very striking example can be found in Senator John McCain's autobiography *Faith of My Fathers*. McCain was a fighter pilot in Vietnam and spent five and a half years in captivity. He writes of being held in solitary confinement:

> It's an awful thing, solitary. It crushes your spirit and weakens your resistance more effectively than any other form of mistreatment. Having no one else to rely on, to share confidences with, to seek counsel from, you begin to doubt your judgment and your courage. But you eventually adjust . . . as you can to almost any hardship, by devising various methods to keep your mind off your troubles and greedily grasping any opportunity for human contact. . . . The punishment for communicating could be severe, and a few POWs, having been caught and beaten for their efforts, had their spirits broken as their bodies were battered. Terrified of a return trip to the punishment room, they would lie still in their cells when their comrades tried to tap them on the wall. [But] very few would remain uncommunicative for long. To suffer all this alone was less tolerable than torture.[5]

Our desire for attention is not a negative thing based on neediness; rather, it is part of what makes us human. It is a reflection of our deep interconnectedness with each other on an energetic level. When all else is stripped away, as in the extreme circumstances McCain describes, sharing energy with another human being can be what keeps us alive.

THE REAL ENERGY CRISIS

How we direct our attention is very important, because it determines where we will "spend" our energy. Gloria Steinem famously said that "We can tell our values by looking at our checkbook stubs." In a world where attention has become the primary currency, I would say that we can tell our values by looking at what we give our attention to. This seems like a simple concept, but it's amazing what problems can be created if we're not conscious of how this works. Where attention goes energy flows, so it's essential to become conscious of our spending habits. Let's look at some of the ways we unconsciously "spend" our attention and how we can begin to correct our errors and regain control of the purse strings of our energy.

Here's a simple example: Have you noticed that if you give all your attention to the TV, you have no energy left to work out, even though all you've been doing is sitting on the couch? And then where do you look to get replenishment? To other people. Be honest—when you feel drained or overwhelmed, don't you look for someone who will give you some attention, knowing that it will make you feel better? In an attention-deprived society, where we all crave attention, what are we really craving? *Energy*. This is the real energy crisis at hand.

Mother Teresa, who devoted her every waking hour to helping people in desperate need of physical sustenance, once said that "there is more hunger for love and appreciation in this world than for bread."

When you want someone's attention you really want their energy. This is why people who are always playing the victim, demanding your attention to listen to their shopping list of woes, drain your energy. It's also why people who are selfless and giving of their attention lift up your spirits when you are near them, leaving you feeling invigorated and refreshed.

There's nothing wrong with exchanging energy with others—that's what relationships are all about. In our interactions with other people, we are always in a dance of energy. And what directs the flow of energy, what choreographs the dance, is our attention. But if we all recklessly spend our attention and therefore our energy on meaningless distractions and then look to each other to get it back, you can see that we will fast create an unsustainable situation. It's like all of us going out with our credit cards and spending thousands of dollars on things we don't need, and then coming to each other and borrowing money to buy food and pay the rent. Sooner or later, we're all going to go bankrupt.

Think about the different people you come into contact with during a day and how these different interactions make you feel. Some people you know may demand a lot of your attention; others may give freely of theirs. When I walk into a room, I like to scan the people present and try to sense where their attention is: Are they giving or taking?

In my relationships—with my colleagues, clients, friends, and family—I gather tremendous insight into the dynamics of attention. All relationships are based on an exchange of energy that is sometimes agreed upon and often times not. For example, think about a budding romance. The two of you meet and your energies connect; you willingly give your partner your attention and your lover freely gives it to you. The exchange of attention is open, honest, and mutual, and you leave each other's company feeling energized.

After a few months, however, perhaps the sparkle has faded. You may find yourself craving the attention of your lover, feeling hurt that you call and he doesn't have the time for you. You may feel like you are competing with your partner's job or friends for his attention. If the situation continues, sooner or later you may lash out at your lover, trying to provoke the attention you have been unable to get. Your partner will all too likely react defensibly because you are now trying to forcefully take energy from him, and a fight ensues. I'm sure you've been in a similar situation in which people use emotional states to protect or get attention. If we weren't all craving attention so much, perhaps we would not have to resort to such games.

It's interesting to compare the energy dynamics in our personal relationships with those in our working relationships. At work we often make a somewhat conscious decision to trade our attention and energy for the money we get paid. When both parties feel like they are getting their money's worth, everything is fine. But if we feel we are not getting paid enough, we either withhold our energy and attention at work or we give much more of it in hopes of getting rewarded with more money. Because many of us want more money, we will sometimes give an enormous amount of energy to work, sometimes to the point where we don't have any energy left when we get home to pay attention to our families. Then you come home feeling drained and craving energy from your spouse, since you left all of yours at work.

Let's play out this scenario a little further—a scenario that was all too familiar to me for many years. You walk through the door to your wife and kids, one being a newborn. Your wife has left her energy and attention on the playroom floor, drained by the constant demands of children. She is craving and expecting attention from you, just as you are craving and expecting it from her. As if it wasn't bad enough that neither of you has any attention left, you are each burdened by each other's expectations. What you really want is to be able to kick back on the couch and have a beer, and for her to provide a sympathetic ear while you complain about what a jerk your boss is. But what she really wants is some help with the kids so she can get one minute to take a shower and wash the baby food out of her hair. When those expectations are not met, too often we withdraw any attention we have left from each other. As the space grows between us, we become reactive in whatever patterns we have learned. Anger, silence, or even alcohol are used to fill the gap that now exists at home. And all of this is the result of not being the master of our own attention. The biggest struggle in a world changing and evolving as fast as ours is to find a way to balance our energy so that we have enough left for all the things that are important to us.

If our attention is so valuable, we obviously need to become conscious of how we are spending it. It's interesting to consider that we're very conscious about how physical activity uses up energy, but we're not so conscious about how mental attention does the same. We would never spend all day running around, from one place to another, without stopping to rest and catch our breath. Yet we let our attention be constantly pulled from one object to the next, and whether we know it or not, our energy goes with it.

Another part of the problem is that often we don't realize how much of our energy is stolen by people around us during the workday—by our attention-demanding coworkers, our clients, even our friends. I realized at a certain point in my life that by the time I got home every day, I had very little energy left to give to the people who needed it the most: my wife and children. My sons would be clamoring for my attention and all I wanted to do was switch my brain off and watch TV. Once I woke up to this pattern of behavior, I learned to conserve my attention during the day and even found ways to boost and empower my own energy through success and creativity, so that when I arrive home now, I have more than enough attention for my family.

If our attention is so valuable, we need to become conscious of how we are spending it.

Recently, I encountered a new and delightful consumer of my attention, in the form of my baby daughter. I soon noticed that my eldest son from my first marriage became withdrawn and seemed to resent and ignore his new sister. His mother and I spoke about it and decided we wouldn't push him, and that we would give him his space. I knew the issue: He was afraid the attention and energy he gets from me would lessen with the arrival of another baby. After a week or two I sat him down and explained the problem as I saw it. I explained how important attention was and how people often manipulated each other so that they could get more of it. I was then able to show him that in his fear of losing my attention he had withdrawn from me in order to defend and protect himself. I proposed that we should work together to pay more attention to each other because that was what we both wanted.

After I had been talking for a little while, he turned to me and said: "You mean people will be nice or mean to you sometimes just to get your attention?" I knew something had really registered with him, and that talk got our relationship back on track. Since that conversation, our whole family seems to have received a boost of energy and everyone feels closer.

MOVING TOWARD WHOLENESS

Have you ever watched a small puppy when it has just been let out into the garden? It will run all over, crossing its own path, following its nose from one scent to another. If you traced its path you would be left with a meaningless, directionless scribble. As long as you are not a master of your attention, you are like that wandering puppy.

Generally speaking, there are three places your attention wanders. The first, as we've been discussing, is outward toward all the things in our world that distract us. But the second consumer of our attention is our own insecure egos—otherwise known as the voice in your head that constantly reminds you of all the reasons you're not already whole and good. That voice says you're not good enough, or you don't yet have all the things you deserve. That voice is really the trigger that causes you to venture outward again and again to try to find the one thing that will quiet that voice once and for all. Whether it's the right job title or relationship or enough money, you are out to prove to that voice that you are okay.

The reason that you'll never find what you need "out there" is because the voice inside will not quit. Over thousands of years of evolution, that voice in our head has performed the job of pushing humanity toward perfection even when we had no clue there was something better. So while it has served an evolutionary function, unfortunately, in our time, this voice can also be our worst enemy.

Although you probably feel quite alone with the voice in your head, I promise you it is one of the things we all share. The people you see in the world who radiate success have just learned to channel that voice into an energy that pushes them toward their creative purpose. And that is the third direction your attention can take: toward creative expression, and toward *others*. We'll be exploring how to do that later in this book, but the first step is just to notice how much of your attention is spent listening to that inner voice and then searching outward for something to quiet it.

||||

> **The reason you'll never find what you need "out there" is because the voice inside will not quit.**

||||

The good news is that you can regain control over your own attention, and not just so that you will feel better at the end of the day. You can begin to harness the extraordinary power of your own attention in such a way that will create much more energy for your work and leave you with plenty of energy to give to those who really need it.

Systems need energy to sustain them. We spend our days involved in much smaller systems, such as our businesses, our families, and our network of friends. And each one of us, by ourself, is also a system. The dictionary defines a system as "a combination of complex things making up a whole." So let's look at the first system you become aware of: *you,* or more specifically, your body. What would your body look like or how long would it survive if you did not give it the proper attention? For the body, this attention translates into the proper amount of food, the right amount of sleep and all the other care and maintenance that a body needs to not just survive but flourish. And we know what happens if we don't give enough attention to caring for our bodies.

Once again, *where attention goes, energy flows.* That's why "the law of attraction" holds true. The basic idea behind the law of attraction—which everyone seems to be talking about these days—is that what you think about is what you attract; what you put your attention on is what you manifest. There's certainly a lot of truth to this principle, although its workings are perhaps a little more subtle than the common New Age translation: "Think positive thoughts and you can have anything you want."

My understanding of the law of attraction is that it is not about using your thoughts to miraculously conjure up what you think will make you happy—that doesn't work even in the movies, for all the reasons discussed in the last chapter. There are a lot of people walking around out there who have read *The Secret* or one of the many other self-help bestsellers that tell you that all you need to do is put your mind on something and it can be yours, and they've done it, and got what they thought they wanted, but they're still caught on the hamster wheel. If, however, you look around you at the people who radiate success, you will see that they are filled with such a clear sense of *purpose* that their attention is not distracted by always trying to get more, but is actually available for responding to the present moment, and to other people.

People crave attention, but the right kind of attention, the unconditional kind that comes with no strings attached. And if energy flows where attention goes, then by giving our attention to others who crave it and to our own creative purpose in the world, we become a vehicle for more energy than we can presently imagine. Take some time to think about attention in some of the ways I've shared in this chapter. Get familiar with this new currency and begin to reflect on your own "spending habits." Throughout the book, I will be referring to attention as the currency for going *beyond success*. I'll show you how to take control of your attention and then use your newfound power source to change your life, achieve your deepest dreams, and even, if you choose, begin to transform the world around you.

My approach to success is all about turning your attention around and realizing that you have an almost unlimited resource that, when used right, can transform people right in front of your eyes. We need to be taught how to get our energy from within and use our attention to begin to heal each other and this planet. Believe me, we can do it, one person at a time. And all it takes to begin is to start to pay attention to where we are putting our attention. I know it sounds almost too simple, but you don't have to trust me—just try it for a short time and see if you don't begin to notice a shift. Countless people I coach tell me that in a very short time it is the one thing that begins to transform their lives. Their relationships get better and the energy to achieve more in the world begins to flow.

IIII

If energy flows where attention goes, we can become vehicles for more energy than we can presently imagine.

IIII

The first step is simply to become aware of how your own attention moves and what directs it. Here are four simple thought experiments you can try as you start to bring light to what may be the most powerful but elusive tool you possess.

1. BODY SCAN. Let's start with an exercise that can help you draw your attention inward, away from the distractions of the surrounding world. Sit somewhere quiet, close your eyes, and focus all of your awareness on your body. Slowly "scan" your attention from your head down to your feet, and see if you become aware of any areas of tension or discomfort. Usually I find that there is some particular area that is storing tension—a knot between my shoulder blades or in the pit of my stomach. As soon as I locate it, I can't believe I hadn't noticed it before. Part of my body is crying out for my attention, but I've been too distracted to notice it. Try this exercise yourself, and notice also how much energy is released when you give your body the attention it wants and learn to release the areas of tension. Just try focusing on the area and imagine yourself breathing into the tension.

2. HOLD FOCUS! Here's a very basic exercise for paying attention. Choose a particular object close to you. It might be a picture on the wall, a coffee mug, or even your own hand. Now put your attention on that object. Don't just stare at it vacantly, but try to direct all of your awareness toward it. Notice the color, the texture, the size, how it makes you feel. Now see how long you can hold that focus, before something distracts you. If you're like most people, this will be a very quick exercise! But it can help to show you, in a simple way, how little we are actually in control of our own attention.

3. EVERYDAY AWAKENINGS. There are many other ways you can begin to become aware of your lack of control over your attention. Think back to your college days and how hard it was not to drift off during those endless lectures. Or perhaps you've had the alarming experience of suddenly realizing, as you are cruising at 70 mph down the freeway, that you can't remember the last five minutes. Becoming aware of moments like these, which happen to us countless times every day, can be the first step toward awakening to a new level of awareness and taking greater control—of not just your car, but the direction of your life.

4. SPENDING REVIEW. This exercise will tell you a lot about why your life is the way it is. Take a piece of paper and draw two axes, like a financial chart or graph. On the vertical axis write the words "low," "medium," and "high." On the horizontal axis write a series of times of day, starting with the time you get up and then adding a point for every hour until you go to bed. Before you go to bed, think back over your day, from the moment you woke up to the moment you are in right now. Try to focus on your energy levels at each significant point of the day. When I say "energy," I don't necessarily mean when you felt the most physically energetic, but when you felt focused, awake, attentive, and most able to cope with whatever situation you found yourself in. Let all the detail blur in your mind so that you just tune in to the energetic element of your experience. It's kind of like that program running on your computer that shows you the output in little bars that spike when the music gets loud and drop down when it softens. For this part of the exercise, you're not interested in what music is playing, whether the melody is beautiful or jarring, you just want to focus on those little bars. For each significant part of your day, "plot" your energy level as high, medium, or low, above the corresponding time. Connect the dots with a line, making a little chart of your energy flow.

Now go back over your day and let the detail come into focus again. Under each point on your energy line, write down what your attention was on at the time. Try to keep it simple: "kids," "TV," "management meeting," "working out." Try doing this exercise for a few days, and then look at the pattern to get a sense of how you are spending your attention—when are you wasting it on irrelevant things and what other parts of your life are suffering as a result. For example, if your energy hits a low point right when you come home from work, you may need to find ways to conserve and generate more energy during the day. If the same person always drains you of energy, you might want to question what that relationship is all about. But don't get too hung up at this point with finding solutions and making changes—the most important step to begin with is to just bring awareness to your attention-spending habits.

CHAPTER THREE

A CORE INVESTMENT STRATEGY

If one is not willing to invest psychic energy in the internal reality of consciousness, and instead squanders it in chasing external rewards, one loses mastery of one's life and ends up becoming a puppet of circumstances.

—*MIHALY CSIKSZENTMIHALYI, Good Business*[1]

AS A FINANCIAL PLANNER, MY JOB IS TO MAKE MAPS. PEOPLE come to me from all walks of life, each with their own unique set of financial circumstances, ideas about money, spending habits, needs, and dreams. But they all come because they want to get from point A to point B. Point A could be anything from a quagmire of debt to a comfortable stipend to a multimillion-dollar inheritance. But point B is always the same: happiness. So my job, at least in theory, is to make them a map to get to a destination called happiness through taking control of their relationship to money.

Now, for all the reasons we've discussed, this plan doesn't really work so well in practice. Not only will money not buy you happiness, but what you think of as "happiness" is probably based on some questionable conclusions about how you'd like to feel all the time. I'm not trying to knock my own profession—taking control of your financial life is a very important step and can definitely help you find more peace of mind and sense of direction. However, the currency of happiness is less tangible than dollars and cents. Time and time again, I have seen clients who got their finances in order but still lacked that sense of deeper fulfillment. And it became clear to me that they were still recklessly spending a far more precious commodity: their attention and energy.

Another way I think about my job is that I'm kind of a financial doctor. People call in a financial planner because they know that their relationship to money is unhealthy. They don't necessarily know the causes, but they are suffering from the symptoms, and they want me to give them a diagnosis and a cure. What I've discovered over the years is that if I'm going to heal their relationship to money, I have to heal their relationship to their own mind. As I learned about the power of attention in my own life, and transformed my relationship to everything, money included, as a result, I began to look at how I could help my clients save, earn, spend, and invest the most valuable commodity they owned.

That's what this book is about. Think of it as "Financial Planning for the Soul," or "An Investment Strategy for Your Attention." There are four pillars of this plan, and each of them can be correlated to a key component of financial wisdom. The financial correlates, however, are not just a metaphor. I don't believe it is possible to have a healthy relationship to money without first having a healthy relationship to your attention. So these pillars are foundational

▮▮▮▮

It isn't possible to have a healthy relationship to money without first having a healthy relationship to your attention.

▮▮▮▮

for financial success, and they can also bring you what money cannot buy. I've discovered in my own experience, and the experiences of the many, many people I have worked with, that following these principles really can get you to a destination worthy of being called Happiness—but it probably won't look or feel like you expected it to!

A FOUR-PART PLAN

My Four Pillars are called:

> **C**onnecting to Source
> **O**wning Your Unique Expression
> **R**edirecting Your Attention
> **E**xpanding Your Awareness

You may notice that the first four letters spell out CORE. I like this acronym, because it connects back to my investing metaphor. Financial planners use the term to refer to the central part of your portfolio: your "core holding." The core requires investments that will be reliable year in and year out—they need to be strong and steady. Having a strong core holding allows you to be creative and take risks with the outer edges of your portfolio without losing your financial balance. Investing your energy and attention in the way these pillars describe is what gives you a "core holding" as a human being—a sense of stability, integrity, wholeness, and purpose that provides a platform for your creativity to flower.

Another reason I like the acronym CORE is that it points to the idea of "core strength." Have you ever been told by a trainer or physical therapist that you need to develop "core strength"? That's why people do all those exercises on large inflatable balls, as you might have witnessed in your local gym, if not tried yourself. The idea is that rather than training isolated muscles like an individual bicep, you work to strengthen those muscles that support everything you do, that keep you stable, balanced, and coordinated, particularly those in your abdominal area and back. It's a more holistic approach to strength training, and one that builds a foundation for continued development.

Many people I meet tell me they feel out of balance, scattered, not whole. And I think a lot of that stems from the fact that we tend to treat the different areas of our life like isolated muscles— our business lives are separate from our spiritual lives, our personal lives are separate from our financial lives. We check our spiritual values at the door when we enter the office, and then wonder why we feel like we are two different people at home and at work.

The Four Pillars are about building core strength, not at the physical level, but at the level of the self. These four principles/practices are like the core muscles of your self-sense, and if you work them out on a daily basis they will provide you with the stability, balance, and coordination to do far more than you could have imagined possible.

Before I explain how these pillars work, I need to tell you a story about where they came from. You see, they weren't something I just sat down and came up with out of the blue. They emerged out of a process that I was going through in my own life, and they were really the result of much soul-searching, risk-taking, and heart-following. This is important, because for these principles to work for you as they do for me, you need to approach them the same way. You can't just apply them superficially to the life you are living and expect instant results. You need to be prepared to engage with them as a process and a practice, and make them your own.

For me, that process began with a longing to integrate my business life and my spiritual life. After I came to the realization that money, in and of itself, would not make me happy, I began to give more and more of my attention to my spiritual interests, hoping to find the fulfillment that material success had not provided. I spent more time meditating, which I had been doing sporadically since I

46

was a teenager, and began to read books on spiritual enlightenment. I started teaching meditation and doing more one-on-one coaching work, because this was where I found the most fulfillment.

My search for integration came to a head for me back in 2005, when I was unexpectedly asked to speak at a weekend business conference. Though happy to participate and share some of what I had learned, I really had no idea what I would say. I didn't see much point in preparing anything, since it was supposed to be a panel-type question-and-answer session. But early Saturday afternoon, I was asked if I could do a solo presentation instead of a panel—and by Sunday, I was to be the closing speaker for the whole weekend.

Somewhat overwhelmed, I went home and mostly meditated. I was alone in my apartment in New York City, with a winter storm raging outside. I just tried to focus my attention, ground it in stillness, and let go of all the anxious thoughts racing through my mind. In the morning, I took a cab to the conference, not realizing how much my life was about to change. I was quite nervous because I didn't know what I was going to say. Before my talk was due to begin, I was in the back of the room doing deep knee bends to try and control my nerves. And that's when I had an image of all this energy flooding into me, and realized that my experience of nervousness was just because I couldn't handle the intensity.

I took a deep breath, got up on stage, and spoke for about forty-five minutes. To my surprise, I was the most confident and the most calm I had ever been when presenting. And as soon as I was speaking, I could see some kind of change happening in the audience. Perhaps "see" is not quite the right word, because it was happening more on an energetic level, but as soon as I started speaking, I palpably felt the energy in the room start to lift.

Now, the only thing I knew, going into that seminar, was that I wanted to talk about attention and energy. I wanted to talk about the fact that underlying everything was a flow of energy, and by paying attention, you could control the energy flow. That was the main theme, but beyond that I had no plan. I just had that one quote from Max Planck about the force that holds together the solar system, because I had heard Wayne Dyer read it on TV that morning while I was eating my breakfast and had written it down on a piece of paper that I tucked in my jacket pocket.

Once I got on stage, I read the quote as a starting point, and then just tried as best I could to think as little as possible. Instead, I focused on this growing feeling that I was doing what I knew I was supposed to be doing and ultimately it didn't matter how it was received. I just let go and got out of my own way.

What came out of my mouth that day was the essence of what this book is all about. My "Four Pillars" emerged on that stage, almost as if I was watching myself from the audience. Of course, it was the culmination of a life process, but this was the moment when it all came together. I knew I'd found the key to what I was put here on earth to do—the means of expression that brought together all the different parts of who I was—what I most deeply desired, what I cared about, what I could contribute.

As I stood there on the stage, my attention was freed up from my nervous, controlling, scrambling mind and I opened myself up to a much deeper current of inspiration and purpose. No longer worried about myself, it became obvious to me that many of the people in the room were experiencing a profound impact, simply because I was giving my attention unreservedly to them.

I walked out of the room knowing that, going forward, my life was going to be based on teaching what had spontaneously come out of my mouth in those forty-five minutes. Since that day, my work has continued to evolve and develop, but those Four Pillars have become the core of the model I teach to thousands of people each year.

CORE INVESTMENT

The Four Pillars are an individual investment plan for your energy and attention. Just like a financial plan, the basic principles are always the same, but they are infinitely customizable to each individual's unique needs and circumstances.

To coach someone through these pillars, I start in the same way as I would begin a financial planning process: I ask about the clients' goals and dreams as well as their current situation and their spending habits. This process helps me serve them, but it mostly helps my clients gain insight into themselves.

Let's reflect for a moment longer on the desire loop, using our financial metaphor. Sometimes the people who come to me for financial guidance have gotten themselves into a downward spiral of debt. Perhaps they started with just one credit card that they used initially for things that they needed. They paid the bills every month. Soon, letters started arriving in the mail from other credit card companies, offering "preapproved" cards at special introductory rates. Before you know it, the person has four or five cards. The original credit card issuer is charging more and more interest, so they get another card to transfer the balance, but keep the original one as well. Soon they can't keep up with all the monthly payments, and then the cards start charging fees as well as interest. It feels like a hopeless cycle, in which money has become their master rather than their servant.

This is a good metaphor for the kind of spiral or loop that many of us get into with our attention. As I described in the previous chapters, when our attention becomes our master rather than our servant, pulling us from one object of desire to the next, we are driven by an endless sense of craving. And when we get the things we thought we wanted, we experience only a brief moment of satisfaction before we find ourselves feeling unfulfilled once again.

Our "seeking brains" crave the thrill that we felt in the anticipation of getting the object of our desire. So we start pursuing another desire, a bigger, better, object. The more we achieve our desires, the bigger the new ones have to be, in order to give us a greater thrill of anticipation than the one before. This is how we get caught in an escalating process, just like the spiral of credit card debt. We become indebted to external objects and internal feelings, unable to extricate our attention from the loop.

The Four Pillars approach this situation the same way a financial planner would approach the debt spiral. The first pillar, *Connecting to Source,* focuses on how we can learn to save our attention, become conscious of how we are spending it, and learn to spend it wisely. Through the practice of meditation, we can break the illusory promise that something "out there" will give us the energy we crave. The first pillar teaches us to connect to an infinite source of energy that we can discover within our very own self.

The second pillar, *Owning Your Unique Expression,* turns to how we earn our energy. Rather than seeking energy from outside ourselves, it helps us to find a mode of *expression* in the world that is a greater source of fulfillment than any object we could possess, because it generates energy as we engage in it. We each have a "unique creative expression," and this pillar can help you discover and own yours, and even make money in the process!

The third pillar, *Redirecting Your Attention,* is about how we invest our energy and attention. It shows us how to invest our attention in who we want to be in the future. I always tell my clients that if you don't invest anything for retirement, it's not going to be much fun when you get there. In the same way, if you are constantly paying the debts of the past or pursuing the desires of the present instead of investing your attention in the future, you are unlikely to get to where you want to be.

The fourth pillar, *Expanding Your Awareness,* is about how we give our energy to others. Many people who come to a financial planner want not only to get their finances in order so they can pay their bills and save for retirement, but they also express a desire to engage in philanthropy, to find a way to give of their wealth to benefit the world. Indeed, many people find that this is what gives them a sense of purpose and meaning. In the same way, when you regain control of your attention, you will find that you have something of tremendous value to contribute that will enrich your life and the lives of all of those you touch.

A NOTE ON HOW TO USE THE FOUR PILLARS

In the chapters that follow, we'll focus on each of these pillars, and I'll explain how you can put them into practice, as well as share stories of how they have worked for me and the people I work with. But first, I'd like to offer a few tips on how you can get the most out of this process.

- **DON'T SKIP PILLAR 1.** A friend asked me, "If you could do only one pillar, which would it be?" I asked him what he thought, and he said, "Pillar 4—at least that way you would be contributing to the world." I disagreed. I would always choose Pillar 1, because unless you are Connected to Source and in control of your attention, whatever you go out and do in the world will not have the impact it could. So take the time to practice Pillar 1, even if it's difficult, and it probably will be. The benefits tend to show up in surprising ways.

- **DON'T GET STUCK ON PILLAR 2.** A lot of people, I have found, get to Pillar 2 and get stuck worrying about what their unique expression might be. There are two ways you can avoid this tendency. First, remember, it doesn't have to be perfect. If you have some sense of direction, follow it, and your creative expression will evolve in the process. However, if you feel like you have no sense of direction whatsoever, I'd suggest you skip Pillars 2 and 3 to begin with, and go straight from Pillar 1 to Pillar 4. Some people find that putting Pillar 4 into practice—expanding their awareness and impact beyond the sphere of their own personal benefit—can be a powerful trigger for discovering what their unique expression actually is. Pillars 2 and 3 are all about having a purpose and direction, but if your purpose has not become clear to you, make it your purpose to learn to harness your attention and contribute to others. You'll be amazed at where it can take you.

■ **PUT THEM INTO PRACTICE.** The Four Pillars are not just intellectual principles; they are practices, so they reveal themselves most deeply through action. I will offer exercises so that you can apply these principles to your own life and experience them for yourself. Don't wait until you feel you understand everything perfectly before trying them. I've found that people's understanding and appreciation of the Four Pillars is something that evolves as they put the principles into practice. Try coming back to the ideas after you have tried the exercises and see if your understanding has developed.

So let's get started on our journey, and look at how you can create a "financial plan for your attention." In the chapters that follow, I'll show you how to build core strength and invest wisely, so that your success becomes not only a source of personal fulfillment but an overflowing wealth of energy and creativity that you share with the world around you.

THE
FIRST
PILLAR

CONNECTING
TO SOURCE

Look well into thyself; there is a source
of strength which will always spring up
if thou wilt always look there.

—*MARCUS AURELIUS ANTONINUS,*
Roman Emperor (AD 121–AD 180)

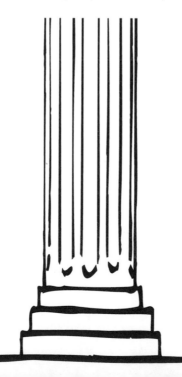

CHAPTER FOUR

SAVING AND SPENDING IN AN ATTENTION ECONOMY

The energy of the mind is the essence of life.
—*ARISTOTLE*

ONE OF THE FIRST PIECES OF ADVICE I GIVE MY FINANCIAL clients is to put away their savings before they do anything else with their paycheck. It's a simple idea, but a very powerful one. I suggest they take 10 percent of their pay and put it in a savings account. Then they can pay their bills, go shopping, or whatever else they would usually do with their paycheck.

The first pillar is about doing the same thing with your attention. Just as most people let their money flutter through their fingers, they do the same thing with their attention, from the moment they wake up until the moment they fall asleep. If you don't find a way to connect to a source of energy and generate a store of energy within yourself, like putting that 10 percent in a savings account, you'll find you don't have enough energy to get you through your day, let alone have any to spare for others.

The good news is, there is a source of power in the universe that we can all plug into. We've just never been taught or trained how to do it. But we've all tasted it, at least for moments. We've all had moments where our minds were rendered quiet by a beautiful sunset, the birth of a child, or by staring into our lover's eyes. These moments give us strength, energy, power. And that power doesn't come from some external thing that our craving minds have grasped hold of. It comes from somewhere deep within, a place we can only access when the mind becomes still.

Look around the room you are sitting in right now and you can probably see a power outlet in one of the walls. Unless you are an electrician, you probably don't really know what happens behind the surface of that wall. But you know that if you plug something into that outlet, it's going to work. Whether it's a blow dryer, a pencil sharpener, a refrigerator, or a computer, plugging it into that power outlet will make it operate. You know that much even if you don't necessarily understand *how* electrical systems work. There is a source of power or energy that is fueling that operation.

The same can be said of human beings, although we rarely seem to feel plugged into that "Source." We are more likely to feel that our energy is being drained out of us. We've all experienced moments of inspiration or creative surges, when we suddenly find access to far greater energy than we usually experience and discover capacities we didn't know we had. In moments like that, we are Connecting to Source. A musician improvising an extraordinary solo in front of a rapt audience, a scientist pursuing a medical breakthrough alone in the lab in the middle of the night, an athlete shattering world records, an aid worker tirelessly saving lives in the middle of a war zone—they are all plugged into the same Source. And each of us channels that same Source in unique ways at different times in our lives.

▌▌▌▌

We've all experienced moments of inspiration when we discover capacities we didn't know we had.

▌▌▌▌

For the purposes of this book, that's all we need to know. If you like to call it God, or Love, or Spirit, or anything else, that's fine, but I use the term *Source* because it takes away a lot of the strongly charged ideas that tend to get associated with such words. It helps to keep it simple—that way we find that we agree far more than we disagree. I think the reason human beings seem to disagree so profoundly about matters of the spirit is that we are always skipping over this simple functional level to try and define the personal attributes of that source or energy. As human beings, we have this tendency to attribute personal qualities to everything, including our spiritual beliefs. But that's where things get very tricky, because we are talking about something we clearly don't fully understand. So, at least temporarily, I'd like to leave aside all our different beliefs about what Source *looks like* and see if we can simply agree that there is a Source. Indeed, if the Source is the essence of everything, then it is the one thing that we all have in common, beyond our belief systems, beyond racial differences and cultural value structures.

PLUGGING INTO OUR POWER

If everything is energy at the deepest level, then the more tuned in you are to the Source of energy in the universe, the more you can actually accomplish. I would go so far as to say that any truly successful person understands how to access this energy to some extent. The simplest way to understand the first principle is that it is about finding a way to plug in, on a daily basis, to access our power.

The more we can quiet our minds and allow space for an open relationship with whatever lies beyond our own "wall," the more that Source seems to fuel us. According to many Eastern systems, the mind is the greatest obstacle to better understanding the world and connecting to the larger energetic system that surrounds us. As we discussed, the mind is bombarded with so many distractions, it's no wonder it can't keep still. The voice in your head is talking so fast you can barely concentrate on anything.

Sometimes I ask people in my seminars to give me an image that describes their mind. "A six-lane highway," one man said. "An endless to-do list," said another. Other images people come up with include an orchestra without a conductor, a jigsaw puzzle with only some pieces joined together, and a traffic jam at a busy intersection. Almost without exception, people come up with images that represent chaos, confusion, fragmentation, complexity, and lack of integration.

IIII

For most of our day, we are not engaging our minds; rather, our minds are engaging us.

IIII

I was recently walking in New York City next to a homeless man who was talking to himself aloud. As crazy as this sight so often seems, it dawned on me that most of us are doing the exact same thing, just silently to ourselves rather than out loud.

Generally speaking, there are two ways our minds work. If you have a project or a task or a problem to solve, you can engage your mind to help you accomplish your goals. A scientist figuring out a lab experiment, a mathematician working out a complex equation, and a writer creating a novel are all engaging the mind in this way. When you engage the mind in problem solving, it is working for you; you are using your mind.

Then there are those times when our minds endlessly chatter. For most of our day, we are not engaging our minds; rather, our minds are engaging us. Your mind may be running around all over the place, depleting your energy and not really accomplishing anything. And during these times, there is probably not much that is useful that your mind is telling you. It's just trying to keep you hooked—on it.

When you are engaging the mind to do a task, you are using the mind. When your attention is caught up in the stream of thoughts, the mind is using you. And as the saying goes, "The mind is a terrible master but a wonderful servant." One of the simplest ways to describe the first pillar is that it is *an opportunity to reclaim your power over your mind* so that rather than your mind holding you captive twenty-four hours a day, seven days a week, you can be the master of your attention.

||||

The first step in learning to harness the power of your attention is to become aware of how it moves.

||||

The first step in learning to harness the power of your attention is to become aware of how it moves. To do this, we need to find a way to disengage from the stream of thoughts that preoccupy us. This is one of the fundamental reasons people practice meditation, in all its many forms. When I use the term "meditation," I don't just mean sitting crosslegged on a cushion, but rather participating in any deliberate activity that teaches us to disengage from a compulsive relationship to the stream of thought.

Although what would traditionally be called meditation is probably the most direct way to harness the power of your attention, there are many other methods as well, and given that we are all unique, each of us should find the method that seems to fit best for us. For some people, it will be the meditation cushion. For others, it might be a nature walk, a kickboxing class, a church visit, or a morning shower (which happens to be my personal favorite). There are numerous books that have been written over the years on the subject of meditation and how to disengage from the thinking mind, or more simply put, *stop listening to the voice inside your head.* It's important that you find a method that works for you. *What* you do is not nearly as important as *how* and *why.*

THE TRUTH ABOUT MEDITATION

You can try meditating right now as you are reading this book. If you pulled your attention away from the words on the page for a minute and watched the thoughts that are going on in your mind, they might go something like this: *I have to go to the bathroom. . . . I don't know why I'm reading this, who is this Jeff Gitterman guy, anyway? . . . I mustn't forget to go to the dry cleaners before six. . . . This is ridiculous, why did I buy his book in the first place? . . . My mother-in-law is coming tomorrow . . . the ball game is on . . . that food smells good. . . .*

Each thought that crosses your mind, you let it go.

If we start to observe our thoughts, we begin to see that they are just fragments, and each one of those fragmented thoughts can be a hook to bring us into a larger, longer, and more drawn out story. Thoughts tend to come in complete sentences, we notice, that can easily string together into paragraphs, and pages, and chapters, and books.

You can create a whole story about that one thought that went by. *That food smells good* leads to further wonderings. *I wonder what's cooking. Gee, my wife is a great cook, I wonder if she's making that broccoli soufflé I love. . . . I'm so hungry . . . but I really shouldn't eat that anyway because I'm supposed to be on a diet. I can't believe I've gained so much weight recently. I really should sign up for the gym again and start going regularly. Otherwise, how am I ever going to fit into that suit for my sister's wedding?* And away we go, down this stream of thoughts.

If you have ever tried to meditate, you have probably discovered for yourself that getting control of your attention is easier said than done. I once read a Zen parable about a monk who arrived in a village, and all the villagers flocked around him asking for the secret of enlightenment. The monk told them: "I can guarantee enlightenment to anyone who can give me their full attention for twenty-four hours." You can probably guess that there were no newly enlightened people the next day. I'm not going to ask you to try the same thing, but let's try a simpler exercise. You can close your eyes if you like, or look at the following blank page, and just for one minute, don't think one thought. Not one.

What you probably found if you tried the exercise is that you can't even stop thinking for a couple of seconds, let alone one minute. Turn back the page and try it for twenty seconds and see if you can do that. The important thing is to be honest with yourself. How long can you go without thinking a thought? My experience is that five seconds is the about the maximum I can go without having a thought of any kind.

To make it a little easier, focus on your breath and count each time you inhale and exhale. See if you can get to twenty without thinking about anything else. Most people who do this, especially the first time, find that they'll get distracted and lose focus by the time they get to the count of three or four. Although this may seem depressing at first, the good news is that reclaiming control of your attention is a very learnable skill, and once learned, you will be able to direct your attention more effectively in ways that you want to.

The power of a practice like meditation is that you get to see how the mind works without acting on any of it. In the usual course of a day, when we grab hold of a random thought and begin to write a story, those sentences would be accompanied by actions. Before you know it, *I'm hungry* becomes a bag of chips or a cookie. *My mother-in-law is coming tomorrow* becomes a fight with your wife over her mother's overly frequent visits. *The ball game is on* leads to forgetting about reading this book, or learning meditation, or anything else that you were previously doing, and flopping down on the couch with a beer.

IIII

You cannot get rid of your thoughts, but you can let go of your *attachment* to them.

IIII

A lot of people I meet think that meditation is a way of learning to stop the mind. In fact, that's the biggest reason most people give up in the early stages. The truth is, it is impossible to turn off your mind.

If you go into meditation thinking you're going to train your mind to stop, you are going to feel very let down and frustrated and unsuccessful very quickly. Stopping the mind is actually not the goal of meditation. The secret to meditation is the discovery that although you cannot get rid of your thoughts, you can let go of your *attachment* to them. You can just let those thoughts continue down the six-lane highway of your mind at a hundred miles per hour and not take them seriously at all.

Meditation reveals to us that there is an alternative to the TV show dramas playing in our heads. It's not that the channel won't be on all the time, but there is an alternative to paying attention to it. You can disengage your attention from it, and even though it may be playing in the background, the volume will have been turned down and, perhaps most importantly, you will have started to find the show it repeats all the time boring.

When you start to be bored by your mind's soap opera, you will find a way to tune in to other channels. And there's a lot going on besides those reruns!

THE MEANS IS THE END

Some people feel that meditation is a waste of time. In our fast-paced modern world, many of us seem to be convinced that unless we're running on the gerbil wheel 24/7, trying to keep up, we are not going to accomplish anything. Yet ironically, even paradoxically, thinking this way actually wastes a tremendous amount of energy. Have you ever seen that guy at the gym who runs from one machine to the next doing exercises very quick and fast, and then he wonders why week after week he has no results? Compare him to the guy who has an incredible physique and does slow, concentrated exercises that really work the muscles. Who's better off in the long run?

Just as we go to the gym to maintain a healthy body, we meditate to maintain a healthy mind. The first few times we go to the gym, it's really difficult and we are sore afterward. But the more we go, the more we find our body is able to perform better and better. We're stronger, we can climb more stairs, we have more energy during the day. With meditation, the more we practice, the more access we gain to the stillness and power that lies beyond our racing minds. Most people are so used to having a final goal in anything they do, whether it is trying to make money, get a promotion, or find a romantic partner. But with meditation there is no end goal. Like taking care of our bodies, it is an ongoing process that yields many benefits but must continually be practiced.

One benefit of learning how to disengage our attention from the thought stream is that we can actually apply our minds to constructive things, such as accomplishing tasks and goals, connecting to other people, seeing what our own true path might be and what we can accomplish in life. It creates space within us—an opening that allows more energy to flow into us. In this seemingly paradoxical way, having more space in our minds allows us to accomplish more and more things in the real world.

I see these benefits so clearly when I look at my own life. If I look back eight or ten years, I realize that although I focused on successfully growing my business, I did so at the expense of my connection to my family, myself, and the world. But in the years since then, as I've trained my mind through meditation, I have gained more energy to accomplish more goals. In the last decade, I've grown a company ten times the size of what it was while also spending time sharing deeper satisfaction and joy with my family. Although I have a lot going on, friends say I'm stiller and calmer today than I ever have been. I have plenty of quiet time and also time for social events. Without question, I attribute this accomplishment directly to my ability to be still through meditation.

Remember, Connecting to Source is not about any one specific practice, and it's not a means to an end—it's the end itself. The most important thing is to learn to spend just fifteen minutes a day, every day, really working with your attention in whatever way is comfortable for you. That will give you a source of energy that will carry you through the rest of your day, helping you be more present, more focused, and more available. This practice brings more success, happiness, and creativity. I guarantee it—if you take the time to try these practices and stick with them, they will bear fruit.

CHAPTER FIVE

PATHWAYS TO SILENCE

Through meditation one realizes the un-
bounded. That which is unbounded is happy.
There is no happiness in the small.
—UPANISHADS[1]

B Y MAKING CONNECTING TO SOURCE A DAILY PRACTICE, ideally something you do first thing in the morning before you start your day, you will begin to see a more natural flow to your life and feel less reactive towards the world. If you've never meditated before, or have tried it a couple of times but not done it consistently, this chapter will offer you a variety of ways to develop a practice that works for you. If you already have a meditation practice, or engage in daily prayer, or have some personal way you like to connect to a deeper silence or stillness, that may work just fine. You can apply the principles of this book to the practice you are already doing. But take a moment to think about whether your practice feels alive and powerful, or whether you have reached a plateau, where the practice has become rote or stale. If it has, consider making changes or trying something different to see if it helps you break through to a new level.

Remember, *what* you do is not nearly as important as *how* and *why*. What matters is that you take some time each day—and it may be just fifteen minutes to begin with—where you consciously watch the thoughts that race through your mind and actively practice not paying attention to them. You may laugh when I tell you that I do my meditation in the shower with the water running, but believe me, with four kids in the house, it is the best place I have found to get the silence I need at the beginning of the day.

WAYS OF MEDITATING

If you are new to the practice of meditation, let's start with the basics. Along the way I'll share a few of my favorite meditation metaphors, both ones I've come up with myself and some that I have learned from others, and use these to illustrate some of the fruits of the practice and the challenges it can present. You can also turn to the list of recommended books on the subject. It's at the end of the book, after the notes. Of course, nothing beats a real live teacher if you feel like you need help getting started. Check your local listings for a meditation class in your area.

I've been practicing meditation for twenty-five years, and teaching it for much of that time also. This chapter contains some of the best examples I've found of meditation techniques. You can adapt them in whatever way works for you, or create your own scenarios, as long as they serve the function of releasing your attention from thought. There are different types of meditation practices that do different things, but for the purpose of Connecting to Source, what I'm asking is that for fifteen minutes every morning, you start learning how to detach your attention from the mind stream. The following practices and visualizations may help you along the way.

SITTING POSITION

It's important that you sit in a position that you can maintain without moving for the duration of your practice. So don't try a full lotus position if you're not an accomplished yoga practitioner—you'll find that after a couple of minutes your legs are screaming and you will have a very hard time not paying attention to the flood of thoughts racing through your head, saying, "I need to move *now*. My leg is numb . . . I don't think this is such a good idea . . . what if I cut off the blood supply to my foot . . . damn this hurts, I need to move *NOW!*"

You can try sitting on a firm cushion with your legs loosely crossed and your back straight, if you find that comfortable. If it's easier for you, sit on a chair. The most important thing is that you are still and alert and not distracted by physical discomfort.

FOCUSING ON THE BREATH

Once you have found a comfortable sitting position, the next step is to focus on your breathing. I recently learned that the word "spiritual" originates from the Latin *spiritualis,* which means *breath*. The process of breathing, which we often don't give a second thought to, is the most basic expression of life. It seems fitting that many forms of spiritual practice are based on observing the flow of this life-sustaining energy source that we exchange with the universe millions of times a day.

The Hawaiians, who greet each other by breathing into each other's noses, created the term *haole* to describe foreigners who didn't know or follow this local custom. Some etymologists claim that this word is derived from "hā'ole," literally meaning "no breath." This claim has been disputed by others, but it is an apt name for many of us who have grown up in Western cultures, because most of us don't know how to breathe.

Try this: *Breathe in.* If you are like most Westerners, your chest probably expanded and your stomach was sucked in. That's what most of us do when we are instructed to breathe in, or take a deep breath. We tend to take only shallow breaths that fill out our chests, but we rarely breathe deep into our bellies, which is what the human body is designed to do.

To meditate deeply, you need to learn to breathe deeply. Your stomach should go out when you take a breath in. Concentrate on filling up your stomach when you breathe, so it expands, and then let it contract as you exhale. Practice this for a few minutes before you try any of the other meditation exercises in this chapter.

Many traditional forms of meditation are based around the breath. Techniques such as Vipassana instruct us to pay attention to our breath, and then notice how often thoughts draw our attention away from the breath. Vietnamese Zen master Thich Nhat Hanh gives the following instructions:

> Your breath should be light, even, and flowing, like a thin stream of water running through the sand. Your breath should be very quiet, so quiet that a person sitting next to you cannot hear it. Your breathing should flow gracefully, like a river, like a water snake crossing the water, and not like a chain of rugged mountains or the gallop of a horse. To master our breath is to be in control of our bodies and minds. Each time we find ourselves dispersed and find it difficult to gain control of ourselves by different means, the method of watching the breath should always be used.
>
> The instant you sit down to meditate, begin watching your breath. At first breathe normally, gradually letting your breathing slow down until it is quiet, even, and the lengths of the breaths fairly long. From the moment you sit down to the moment your breathing has become deep and silent, be conscious of everything that is happening in yourself. . . .

Try paying attention to your breathing in this way, so that it can help you focus. If it is too difficult in the beginning, Thich

Nhat Hanh also suggests that you count your breaths until you train your mind to rest without too much distraction.

> As you breathe in, count 1 in your mind, and as you breathe out, count 1.
> Breath in, count 2. Breath out, count 2.
> Continue through 10, then return to 1 again.[2]

USING OTHER POINTS OF FOCUS

Other traditional aids to meditation include a string of beads called a mala, which you can use to count your breaths or repetitions of a mantra. A mantra is a simple phrase that you can repeat in order to focus your concentration and break the grip of the chattering mind. In many traditions, the most basic mantra is "Om" or "Aum," representing the indivisible One reality. You can choose a traditional phrase if you like, such as the Tibetan "Om mani padme hum." According to the Dalai Lama, this mantra promises that by practicing a path of skillful activity and wisdom, you can transform your impure body, speech, and mind into the pure exalted body, speech, and mind of a Buddha.[3] The Hindu mantra "Aum shanti shanti shanti" invokes a sense of peace. Some schools of Christianity espouse the practice of contemplative prayer or "breath prayer." Best-selling author and pastor Rick Warren advises readers of *The Purpose-Driven Life* to "choose a brief sentence or a simple phrase that can be repeated to Jesus in one breath: 'You are with me.' 'I receive your grace.' . . . You can also use a short phrase of Scripture."[4] Find a mantra or prayer that has meaning for you, or create your own simple, powerful phrase.

Whatever you choose to focus your attention on, the most important thing to remember is to keep it simple: don't create elaborate rituals that can provide another distraction for the mind. Sometimes I like to meditate by focusing on a candle flame, because it reminds me of this beautiful line from the Bhagavad Gita: "When meditation is mastered, the mind is unwavering like the flame of a lamp in a windless place."

PICTURES OF STILLNESS

When I think about Connecting to Source through meditation, the best image I can find to describe it is that of a well. The well represents your mind. At the top of the well you see some clear water. And then if you look past that surface, the water gets murkier, and beneath that, there are layers of sediment, which represent thoughts, feelings, cultural beliefs, and psychological structures. These layers go down through the well, getting darker and denser and more compacted as you go deeper. At a certain point the sediment may get so thick that it seems like the bottom of the well, but it's important to know that the well actually reaches all the way to the molten core of the earth, which is a ball of light and heat and energy. That molten core represents Source.

When we practice meditation, it's like taking one layer at a time, stirring up the sediment, and clearing it away. You will find that you get more clear water near the top, which represents the clarity of your attention. When people begin to meditate, usually what happens is that they get some clarity and some sediment cleared out and they feel like they've made a breakthrough. Then after a little while—it can be hours or days or weeks or months— as they are enjoying that feeling of clarity, they hit another layer of sediment that makes things murky again. People often get frustrated and quit meditating when this happens, because they think they have "lost" that breakthrough that they had imagined would be permanent. But that's not the case. They have just reached a deeper layer. And these layers are basically stuck patterns, beliefs, and thoughts about yourself and your world that may have been lockcd away since childhood and never really examined.

I use metaphors to describe the practice of meditation because it is an intangible experience, and that makes it very difficult to pinpoint or describe directly. Adding to this challenge is the fact that when meditating, it is very important not to get hung up on any particular notion of what it is supposed to look or feel like. As explained in the previous chapter, there is no specific end goal, and no "right way" to do it. Metaphors don't fix the experience in place or define the way things "should" be—they keep the experience fresh, which prevents us from getting stuck in a stale or rote routine.

IIII

When we practice meditation, it's like taking one layer at a time, stirring up the sediment, and clearing it away.

IIII

Once again, the point of meditation is not to rest in light and clarity and peace forever. Meditation is a constantly unfolding process. I really believe that as long as you are practicing meditation, and are doing it with earnestness, you'll always keep hitting new layers in which you're stuck. If you are open to that process, it is going to enrich your life because meditation, when practiced regularly, can help to ground and focus your attention in ways that few, if any, other endeavors can. But it's not going to be easy. In fact, oftentimes meditation can be very uncomfortable, because it stirs up things that you may not want to see in, or know about, yourself. The key to meditation is not to get caught by any of the pieces of sediment that are rising to the surface.

Try not to get discouraged if you feel like you're stuck. Let's use the comparison of going to the gym again. If you've ever worked out with any consistency, you probably know what it's like to hit a plateau. For most people, after a few weeks, they look in the mirror and think, "Wow, I look different." This is a breakthrough.

Inspired, they step up the pace and start working out harder and going to the gym more often. And then, about three or four months later, you look in the mirror and it seems like nothing is changing. You've reached a plateau. And if you consult a trainer or professional athlete, usually they will encourage you to change your routine or make it more challenging in order to have a new breakthrough that takes you to an entirely new level of fitness.

Returning to the well metaphor, the most important thing is that as those layers begin to break up and become dislodged; the light of that molten core begins to break through into your awareness. All that sediment may not go away, it may keep floating around in the water of the well, but the light and energy of Source is able to permeate all the way to the surface of your life.

THE STREAM MEDITATION: BE GENTLE WITH YOURSELF

One of my favorite ways of meditating is what I call the stream meditation. Start by imagining yourself sitting in a paradise garden—I like to think it's the Garden of Eden. It's a beautiful day, with a warm breeze and the scent of spring dancing in the air. It's completely silent, except for the sound of a stream that is flowing in front of you. You sit down, cross-legged, on the grassy bank, right by the water's edge. Take a deep breath, all the way down into your stomach, and slowly exhale. When a thought arises in your mind, imagine that it is a stick or a log or even a tangle of branches that you just drop into the stream and let float by.

If you are a beginner you may find that during meditation, every five seconds you can let go of one thought, and let go of another thought, but by the time the third or fourth thought pops into your head, you start following one of those thought-sentences until soon you've created a whole story. It's like jumping into the stream, grabbing hold of one of those logs, and being carried along by the current. One minute you were sitting on the bank of the stream watching every thought go by, then this one thought looked really attractive, you got caught by it, and it carried you away.

A sentence can become a story very quickly. The first thought might be, *Does my Garden of Eden look right?* And then the next one: *How do I know what the Garden of Eden should look like, anyway? I really have an itch. I should scratch it. Do I really think there ever was a Garden of Eden?* And before you know it, you're having a debate in your mind. *I don't really believe in the Garden of Eden, I'm not a very religious person. Maybe I shouldn't be trying this meditation. I know, I'll go to the library and look for a different meditation book. Oh, that reminds me, my library books are overdue. Damn, I always forget. . . .* And there you go, hanging on to the log, floating down the stream.

And when you notice what's happened, when sooner or later that thought comes by—*Oh, I'm supposed to be meditating*—you need to bring yourself back to the side of the stream and continue to watch the logs go by. At moments like that, it's important to be very gentle with yourself, because meditation is not a judgmental process. You just need to gently remind yourself that you want to be sitting by the side of the stream letting go of each thought. And remember, *Oh, I'm supposed to be meditating* is a thought, too. It might remind you that you are meant to be sitting on the bank, and that's good. But you have to let that thought go immediately, or it can start a story of its own. *Oh, I'm supposed to be meditating. . . . Dammit, I got lost again. . . . I am such a useless meditator . . . I wish my mind would just slow down. . . . So-and-so from my yoga class says that every time she meditates she feels overwhelmed by bliss and peace . . . how come I don't feel like that? . . . Maybe I should forget about this meditation thing . . . my butt hurts. . . .* This time you've been carried miles down the stream.

If you are new to meditation, you'll probably find that four or five thoughts later you'll be back in the stream hanging onto a log.

And while this might seem like a silly process, what it is allowing you to do is train your attention to disengage from an addictive attachment to thought. A while ago, my wife was trying the stream meditation. And after a few minutes, she called me up and said, "I can't do this! My thoughts aren't just sticks floating on a stream—it's a flood, and there are branches, trees, the dam, the whole village, coming down the hill and I'm sitting here trying to pick out individual thoughts." When she said this, I was reminded of what a powerful practice it is to even begin to differentiate thoughts from the tumult of the untamed mind. Until we begin meditation practice, we are not even aware of thoughts as distinct from one another. So, as I told my wife, just start with that. Begin to notice where one thought begins and ends.

||||

Meditation, in its most successful form, is a very gentle thing. If you encounter difficulties, they should not cause you to judge yourself.

||||

In so doing, you are taking an important step towards making space in your mind for Source to be able to access your mind, to create more inspiration, more creativity, and more energy. In the beginning, when you find yourself drifting in the stream over and over again, in all probability you're going to get frustrated. So *be gentle with yourself.* In the beginning, meditating is not much fun. I find this one of the most challenging parts of the practice. As soon as I lose my focus, my mind says, *Oh God, get back on the bank. Focus, focus, focus.* I start to beat myself up. *I suck. What a terrible meditator I am.* And that's just another thought that is attractive because we are so used to judging ourselves.

Meditation, in its most successful form, is a very gentle thing. The difficulties you come across as you begin to practice aren't something to add judgment onto yourself about; we already have enough judgment and criticism in life. You just gently remind yourself that you are supposed to be sitting on the side of the stream, not floating in the stream, and you bring yourself back. The analogy that is often used is that of a baby learning to walk. In the process, the baby falls down many times. But the baby doesn't say, "What's the matter with me? Boy, am I a crappy walker." She doesn't judge herself at all, but simply keeps trying to walk. She is willing to fall down as many times as she needs to until she learns. If we could take this attitude with us as we start to meditate, we will find that we can progress much faster. Remind yourself frequently that in meditation, there is no goal to reach and no target to hit. If you fall into the trap of thinking the goal is to stop your mind, you are guaranteed frustration. In meditation, what we are cultivating is a state in which we are able to watch thoughts without attaching ourselves to them. Tibetan teacher Sakyong Mipham describes this experience as "placement." In *Turning the Mind into an Ally,* he writes:

> Each time you choose to recognize and acknowledge a thought and return your consciousness to the breath, you are learning placement. It's such a small act, so innocuous, but it's one of the most courageous things you can do. When you recognize and release that thought, you can take pride in yourself. You've overcome laziness. You've remembered the instructions. You can feel happy coming back to the breath. Don't worry that you're going to have to do it again—you're going to do it thousands of times. That's why it is called practice.[5]

TRAIN OF THOUGHT

Another way of meditating that a lot of people find useful is the train meditation. I often add my own variations, but this metaphor comes from Steven Levine, who wrote *A Gradual Awakening,* one of the best books for beginning meditators. This meditation technique led to some of my biggest breakthroughs in understanding that my random thoughts were responsible for creating my emotional states, and that realization was key to gaining control over my emotions.

> An image about practicing meditation that may be helpful is that of standing at a railroad crossing, watching a freight train passing by. In each transparent boxcar, there is a thought. We try to look straight ahead into the present, but our attachments draw our attention into the contents of the passing boxcars: we identify with the various thoughts. As we attend to the train, we notice there's supper in one boxcar, but we just ate, so we're not pulled by that one. The laundry list is the next one, so we reflect for a moment on the blue towel hanging on the line to dry, but we wake up quite quickly to the present once again, as the next boxcar has someone in it meditating and we recall what we're doing. A few more boxcars go by with thoughts clearly recognized as thoughts. But, in the next one is a snarling lion chasing someone who looks like us. We stay with that one until it's way down the line to see if it got us. We identify with that one because it "means" something to us. We have an attachment to it. Then we notice we've missed all the other boxcars streaming by in the meantime and we let go of our fascination for the lion and bring our attention straight ahead into the present once again.[6]

After you have been meditating for a couple of weeks, you will begin to have some distance from the endless movement of your mind, and you will probably start to notice certain patterns. You will see that you tend to have certain kinds of thoughts, and certain feelings about those thoughts.

This is where you can add another element to the process. Try to come up with three or four main types of thoughts—they might be worry-thoughts, fear-thoughts, happy-thoughts, and sad-thoughts. Stay with a few broad categories to begin with, otherwise they will become another thing for your attention to latch onto. Begin your meditation as before, but as you place each thought in its box, give it a label. You can do the same thing with the stream meditation. Each thought that pops into your head is something that you label and place in the box or drop in the stream.

What this process allows you to do is see the randomness of the thought fragments that come into your mind. They come in no particular order—worry-thought, sad-thought, happy-thought—they just arise randomly. And you will start to notice that whichever thought you start creating the story around has a dramatic effect on your actual emotional state—all because of the tag that's attached to that random thought. So this process reveals how your emotional state is reactively moving throughout the day, based on completely random thoughts in your mind.

THE BOOKSTORE MEDITATION

Bookstores fascinate me. There is something about the ideas of so many people put in one place for our enjoyment that calms me to the core. I came up with a meditation that works very well for me one day when I was browsing through my local Barnes and Noble. You know what it's like when you walk into a bookstore. All these book titles are popping out at you until sooner or later you see one that really attracts you. Before you know it you have walked over to the bookshelf and opened that book. Well, the human mind kind of works the same way. Imagine yourself in a huge library or bookstore. Everywhere you look there are shelves stretching in all directions, from floor to ceiling—thousands and thousands of books. It's dark in the bookstore because you are there alone after closing time. You sit down cross-legged in the middle of the store and turn all of your attention inward.

Now imagine that each thought that pops into your head is a book title that almost lights up like a neon sign on the shelf. Perhaps a book called *I Have to Go to the Bathroom* catches your eye on shelf three. You let that go and bring yourself back to sitting in the center of the bookstore or library. Then *My Credit Card Is Overdue* lights

||||

The bookstore meditation shows you how any particular thought that pops up has an entire story in it.

||||

up on a shelf over to your right. And you just keep letting it go. The next moment a big red title catches your attention: *I Don't Get Why My Wife Was Mad at Me This Morning*. Before you know it, you are standing in front of the shelf and you're already on page twenty of a very absorbing story.

The great thing about this meditation is that it shows you how any particular thought that pops up has an entire story in it. If you latch on to that thought, it is as if you've taken the book off the shelf and started reading a story about how *I Have an Itch on My Back,* or how *I Can't Pay My Bills Today,* or how *No One Loves Me*. And your mind has its own best-seller list, you will notice. So what you want to do is just gently put the book back on the shelf and remind yourself that now is not the time to be reading. Go back to sitting quietly, in the middle of the bookstore.

THE SUBWAY MEDITATION

American spiritual teacher Andrew Cohen grew up in New York City, and he has a metaphor for meditation that any New Yorker or other city dweller around the world will be able to relate to:

> I grew up in Manhattan and I started taking the subway when I was nine years old. My mother told me: don't talk to strangers, even if they talk to you.
>
> As anyone who rides the subway regularly knows, there are a lot of strange, crazy people hanging out in the subway, and those people want something from you. Sometimes they want money, sometimes they want to sell you something, but often they just want attention.

Now, what do you do if you see a crazy man coming toward you, talking to himself? Be honest—you ignore him, don't you? You see him, but I'm sure you have discovered that you can actually freeze him out. You don't make eye contact, you don't respond, you act as if he did not exist. Why do you do this? Because you know that the minute you acknowledge his existence, even through eye contact or saying "no" or trying to get him to leave you alone, you will have gotten into a relationship with him, and once he has your attention, it is very hard to extricate yourself. So although you can't make the crazy guy disappear, you choose, through your own volition and will, to have no relationship with him. You can do exactly the same thing with your thoughts.[7]

In this way, meditation becomes the vehicle by which we free ourselves from relationships that don't serve us—unhealthy, compulsive relationships with our own thoughts and feelings. This begins by learning not to listen to the crazy ideas within us that constantly vie for our attention, any more than we'd choose to listen to a crazy guy on the subway.

OTHER VISUALIZATIONS

Here are some other metaphors that you might find useful.

THOUGHT BUBBLES

You know how in a cartoon strip, thoughts and speech are represented by bubbles that float in the air over the character's head? For the period in which you are meditating, imagine you are sitting in one frame of a cartoon strip. There are no frames that come after the one you're in. You are in the present moment. And so each time a thought-bubble arises, let it float out of the frame, making space for a new one to appear without you moving from your seat.

WAVES ON THE OCEAN, RIPPLES ON A POND . . .

Many meditation teachers use metaphors like the ocean, or a pond, or a lake. Imagine that your mind is like calm, flat water. Thoughts may arise, like ripples or wavelets or even crashing waves, but they always die down again and merge back into the smooth surface. The idea is to keep your attention on the ocean or the pond as a whole, and not get distracted by the movements on the surface.

YOU'VE GOT MAIL!

I came up with a new metaphor the other day as I was sitting at my computer trying to write this book. Think of it as a meditation metaphor for the digital age! If you spend much time at a computer, your e-mail program probably sends you notifications every time new mail arrives in your in-box. Older programs used to just play a sound or a beep, and then a little envelope would appear in the bottom corner of your screen My upgraded e-mail program, however, uses notification messages that appear on the screen as translucent little boxes that float to the surface, showing me the tantalizing first sentence of the e-mail that has just arrived. So perhaps I am sitting there trying to write, focusing on the task at hand, when I hear "bing" and a little box floats into focus, telling me:

FROM: FRED
SUBJECT: GREAT NEWS!
HEY JEFF, I HAVE SOME FANTASTIC NEWS . . .

If I ignore the little box, it will fade away and disappear, leaving just the little envelope icon to remind me of my waiting mail. If I'm tempted to read it, and roll my mouse so that the cursor touches it, miraculously the translucent box becomes solid. And if I click it, it takes me directly to my waiting message and to Fred's fantastic news that he has just gotten engaged and hopes I will be able to come to the wedding, which will be in California in June . . . and then I check my calendar and call my wife and my writing is long forgotten.

This is what thoughts are like in meditation. They float to the surface with a tantalizing sentence, and if we "click" them, before we know it we are lost in a long message and all its repercussions. But if we simply observe their arising without moving, they will start to fade away again like those e-mail notifications.

A MIND LIKE THE SKY

Here is another meditation I like, from American Buddhist teacher Jack Kornfield. In an article for *Shambhala Sun* magazine, entitled "A Mind Like the Sky: Wise Attention, Open Awareness," he offers instructions for practicing an "opening" approach to the mind:

> One of the most accessible ways to open to spacious awareness is through the ear door, listening to the sounds of the universe around us. Because the river of sound comes and goes so naturally, and is so obviously out of our control, listening brings the mind to a naturally balanced state of openness and attention. . . .
>
> As you listen [to the play of sounds around you], let yourself sense or imagine that your mind is not limited to your head. Sense that your mind is expanding to be like the sky—open, clear, vast like space. There is no inside or outside. Let the awareness of your mind extend in every direction like the sky.
>
> Now the sounds you hear will arise and pass away in the open space of your own mind. Relax in this openness and just listen. Let the sounds that come and go, whether far or near, be like clouds in the vast sky of your own awareness. The play of sounds moves through the sky, appearing and disappearing without resistance.

As you rest in this open awareness, notice how thoughts and images also arise and vanish like sounds. Let the thoughts and images come and go without struggle or resistance. Pleasant and unpleasant thoughts, pictures, words, and feelings move unrestricted in the space of mind. Problems, possibilities, joys, and sorrows come and go like clouds in the clear sky of mind.[8]

WALKING MEDITATION

Some people find sitting still on a cushion uncomfortable, and others find it unbearable, for a variety of reasons. If so, you might want to try a form of walking meditation that is practiced in many spiritual traditions. If practiced seriously in a quiet place, walking meditation can be just as powerful as sitting meditation, and it may be easier to incorporate into your daily life. It allows you to be more present in your body and in the present moment.

Just as with sitting meditation, it is important to set aside a specific time for walking meditation, even if it is only fifteen minutes. Don't try to combine it with running errands or exercise, but give your full attention and intention to the practice. I like to do it outdoors, although a quiet sacred space like a church can also be a good venue as long as you are not disturbing others. You can even circle your living room.

Before you start walking, focus on your breath in the same way that you would to begin a sitting meditation. Let your awareness follow your breath, in and out, calming and focusing you before you begin walking. Once you are ready to begin, start slowly walking, keeping your movements gentle and relaxed, and let the rhythm of alternating between the right foot and the left foot help you settle into a meditative state. Try to keep your eyes down or let your vision blur a little so that you don't become distracted by anything in your visual field. If you do find your attention getting caught by your surroundings, just bring it back to the rhythm of walking and breathing.

The basic idea with walking meditation is that the physical experience of walking can provide something for you to focus on as a means of taking your attention away from thought. As you walk, pay attention to the sensations in your body. Notice how walking is not just something you do with your legs, but something you do with your whole body. If you find it helpful, you can start at the soles of your feet and slowly move up through your entire body. Release any areas of tension. Every time you get caught up in the thought stream, bring your attention back to the act of walking.

COMMON OBSTACLES TO MEDITATION

There are many reasons people get stuck, derailed, or discouraged in the practice of meditation. Here are a few common ones to watch out for:

▌ **MIND COMBAT.** It's not a good idea to let yourself get into a battle with your mind. The mind thrives on energy. If you resist it, you actually feed it and give it energy. So avoid meeting your mind with resistance. Rather than sitting down to meditate with the idea that you are going to conquer your mind, just sit and let it be, and you will find that your mind calms down by itself if you don't fuel it with the resistance. Remember, if you are fighting with the mind, it has already won.

▌ **THINKING YOU DON'T HAVE TIME.** A lot of people think they don't have time for meditation. But when you begin to appreciate its value, and realize how much it liberates your attention and creativity, you will begin to understand that you do not have time *not* to meditate. As Milarepa, one of Tibet's legendary yogis, is said to have told people: "The affairs of the world will go on forever. Do not delay the practice of meditation."

▋ **DEALING WITH OLD WOUNDS OR SCARS.** Meditation can be a cleansing experience, but the process can sometimes bring to the surface old psychological and emotional wounds and scars that you find difficult to bear. In the practice of meditation itself, it is important not to get caught up in trying to deal with these issues, but just to let them go like any other thought. However, you may find that in conjunction with your meditation practice you want to spend some time with a therapist who can help you begin to heal these wounds from the past, leaving you more free in your meditation practice not to worry about such matters.

▋ **SPIRITUAL PRIDE.** Some people obtain a sense of spiritual power from meditating—which is also something to be avoided! Meditation is about your own personal relationship with Source; it's not something you should use to feel superior to others.

▋ **EXPERIENCE ADDICTION.** If you take the practice of meditation seriously, sooner or later you will probably experience peace, bliss, oneness, or energetic currents running through your body, like the powerful white light of *kundalini*. But even if you have powerful experiences, you have to let those go, too. Many people try to make deeper meaning of them and lose their meditative awareness through a fascination with the experience. And the most common problem with good experiences is that once we have one, we want to have more. Our meditation practice, then, becomes another form of craving, a kind of spiritual consumerism or addiction to higher states of consciousness.

Don't look for the highs—instead, seek steadiness and consistency. As the Indian sage Patanjali said in the Mahābhāsya, "In deep meditation the flow of concentration is continuous, like the flow of oil." Always remember, the purpose of meditation is to let go of all thoughts—and that means everything.

▌ **GOAL FIXATION.** For those of you who have meditated for years, or feel that you are on some journey toward the destination known as Enlightenment, it's important to remember that even Enlightenment is not a fixed destination. Meditation is an end in itself, not a means to an end.

▌ **BOREDOM.** A lot of people I meet tell me that they took up meditation at some point or other in their lives, but found it difficult to stick with it because they got bored or frustrated. Many people even find that the minute they sit down to meditate, they fall asleep. I think in many cases this happens because people begin the practice without having a clear idea of the purpose it is designed to achieve. Boredom is actually a good thing. It means you are getting tired of your thoughts and aren't as caught up in them. So think of boredom as a sign that the practice is working, and continue on!

Remember, meditation is a *practice,* which means you have to stick with it to see the benefits. It may take discipline to set aside those fifteen minutes every morning, but trust me, it will pay off. Meditating before you begin your day will help you save energy for when you really need it, and it will also help to liberate you from your craving mind, allowing you to spend your attention more wisely throughout your day.

THE
SECOND
PILLAR

OWNING YOUR
UNIQUE EXPRESSION

If a man is called to be a street sweeper,
he should sweep streets even as
Michelangelo painted, or Beethoven
composed music, or Shakespeare wrote
poetry. He should sweep streets so well
that all the hosts of heaven and earth
will pause to say, here lived a great street
sweeper who did his job well.

—*MARTIN LUTHER KING*

CHAPTER SIX

EARNING ENERGY

Everything—a horse, a vine—is created
for some duty. . . . For what task, then, were
you yourself created? A man's true delight
is to do the things he was made for.

—*MARCUS AURELIUS, Meditations*[1]

HUNDRED YEARS AGO, IT WOULD HAVE BEEN PRETTY EASY to tell a person's income level and social status at a glance. All you would have to do was look at the quality of the clothes they were wearing, the jewelry or other luxuries they displayed, the shoes on their feet, the house they lived in, and the way they traveled. But today, that's all changed. As a financial planner, I know better than most that in this age of multiple credit cards and multiple mortgages, a person's lifestyle can bear little or no relationship to their income.

I can show up for a meeting with a new client, park next to his sleek sports car, admire his manicured lawn and beautiful house, and notice his Rolex when he shakes my hand. But when I begin to delve into his financials, I find that although he has a reasonable income, it is nowhere near what would be needed to fund the lifestyle he is living. It's no surprise when he tells me he has maxed out his credit, double-mortgaged his house, and isn't saving anywhere near enough for retirement. This guy is a classic example of what they call "living beyond your means."

I might go to meet another new client, however, and find her living in a modest house, driving a well-cared-for but well-used car, and wearing a watch that cost less than $100. When I begin to look into her financials, I find that she has the exact same income as the first client. But she has a substantial amount saved for retirement and is living comfortably within her means. Ironically, I'll often find that this client is a lot more satisfied with her life and experiences more peace and joy than the guy who has all the gadgets.

Unfortunately, in our consumer-driven culture, living beyond one's means has become an acceptable practice that we don't think twice about it. As comedian Will Rogers said, "Too many people spend money they haven't earned, to buy things they don't want, to impress people they don't like." Kids are overspending before they are even out of school. Seventeen-year-olds spend their student loans on designer clothes and iPhones and don't think twice about it. According to the College Board, during the 1990s, the average student-loan debt doubled; by 2004, the average college graduate was starting his working life with a debt of $17,600.[2] Many people I know don't pay off their student loans until they are well into their thirties.

> **In financial matters, you cannot live beyond your means. The same is true when applied to the currency of attention and the energy it carries.**

One of the most basic pieces of advice that any financial planner worth his salt will give you is that you cannot afford to live beyond your means. This seems like an obvious point when it comes to money, but in many ways it's just as true when we apply it to the currency of attention and the energy it carries with it.

If you have been trying some of the exercises from the previous chapters, you will no doubt have started to observe that there are certain activities that seem to drain your energy and others that seem to give you energy. Another way to look at the situation, to continue our financial metaphor, is that certain activities require an expenditure of energy while others seem to earn energy. And it's not just that restful activities give you energy and more stressful or demanding ones drain it. I'm sure there are things that you love to do that might be physically, mentally, and emotionally challenging but leave you feeling energized and rejuvenated.

The second pillar, Owning Your Unique Expression, helps you to identify those activities or modes of expression that earn you the greatest amount of energy. Only then can you begin to align your life and, in particular, your work with those sources of energy income.

I believe that every one of us has a unique creative expression that is, to put it simply, *the thing we are here to do.* Since I was a little kid, I've always had this underlying sense that there was something specific in life I was supposed to be doing. Many people I meet tell me they feel the same way. But often they're not sure exactly what it is. Sometimes they have something they love to do but don't have much time or energy to devote to it because they're too busy making a living. Or some people are working in a job they love, but are constantly worried because it doesn't pay the bills. As a financial planner, I meet a lot of people who are retiring, and I have noticed that sometimes people discover a whole new sense of meaning and purpose in the last part of their lives and wish they could start over. What all these people have in common is a belief, often reinforced through their life experience, that being financially successful and doing what they love are somehow incompatible. We may see others who have a "gift" or talent that they love and who are able to make money from it, but these individuals seem like the exception rather than the rule.

I am convinced that not only *can* we make a living with our unique expression; in fact, it is the *only* way we can be truly successful. I remember reading a story about an attorney who made about a half million dollars a year, but she really hated her job. Yet she was so fearful of letting go of the money that she kept working at the same job, feeling stressed, overwhelmed, and unfulfilled, until a coach came along and said, "If you're making so much money doing something you hate, just imagine how much more money you could make doing something you love!"

When you start to look at your choice of work in terms of how you are spending your most precious commodity, you will realize that you really cannot afford to be doing a job that does not energize you and fill you with a sense of purpose. It is often estimated that the average adult will spend 80 percent of his waking life at work. If you are spending all that time in a job you hate, one that drains your energy and attention so that you have none left for the remaining 20 percent of your life, then we could say that energetically you are living beyond your means. You'll find yourself needing to get energy back from the people around you, particularly those you love, and you'll have very little left to give.

Many people justify such a lifestyle from a financial standpoint and tell themselves they will reap the rewards when they retire. But I would argue that fantasies of sitting poolside and playing golf in the twilight of our lives may not be as fulfilling as we think. I work with hundreds of retirees, and it is a rare person who really enjoys a life of full leisure. Many retirees become depressed without purpose and often return to the workforce, not out of financial need, but in search of a greater sense of meaning. Or they just get the job so they can have their evenings and weekends free. But the problem is, you still have to do the job, and you'll probably spend more time doing the job than you will have left in retirement or in the evenings and on weekends. On the level that really counts, the math doesn't add up.

As Richard Branson, founder of Virgin Group and one of the most successful and out-of-the-box businessmen of our time, said in an interview with *Money* magazine, "If you're into kite-surfing and you want to become an entrepreneur, do it with kite-surfing. . . . If you can indulge in your passion, life will be far more interesting than if you're just working. You'll work harder at it, and you'll know more about it." Branson describes how his first business venture came out of a desire to be the editor of a magazine. At the age of sixteen, he felt passionately about communicating to other students, so he founded a magazine. He became a businessman by accident because he wanted to make sure his magazine would survive. "Most businesses fail," he says. "So if you're going to succeed, it has to be about more than making money."[3]

Owning Your Unique Expression takes this approach to the arena of life in which we spend most of our time. It's not just about making money—it's also about earning energy. I like the financial metaphor of "earning" something, but in a sense it is paradoxical, because the way we earn energy is not through a process of *taking* but actually through a process of *expression*. What we find is that there is no greater source of energy and inspiration than the sense that we are fulfilling our own purpose, doing the thing that we are put here on earth to do.

Most activities we engage in *require* energy. Even sitting at a desk all day can leave you drained. But sometimes we find something that seems to actually *give* us more energy the more we do it, even though it appears that it would take energy to engage in it. That's when time seems to pass without us even noticing. We feel we could keep going forever, and we look forward to the next opportunity we have to engage in whatever activity it may be. It might even be an activity that is very demanding and stressful—like working in an emergency room or playing a sport. But the key here is that the activity itself is what gives fulfillment.

Often we are only willing to give our energy in order to get something in return—whether it be money or attention or status. But when you find your unique creative expression, you will dis-

▌▌▌▌

Sometimes we find activities that actually generate more energy the more we do them.

▌▌▌▌

cover that the act of doing it is its own reward. Your unique creative expression is the way that Source expresses itself through you. As we discussed, Source is where energy comes from. When you feel that sense of being fueled from within, it is a sure sign that you are connecting to that deeper source of energy. Then you will no longer be constantly seeking for energy from other people and the world around you, but will be giving energy to others at the same time that you are energizing yourself.

When I say "unique creative expression," I don't necessarily mean some special talent. It doesn't mean you have to be a concert pianist or an Olympic athlete or the one to find a cure for cancer. Many of us who have grown up in the second half of the twentieth century, i.e., the boomer generation and their kids, have had a tremendous amount of freedom to shape our own lives the way we want to. We have a seemingly endless array of options, a freedom of choice that our grandparents could never have even dreamed of. And this is a great gift of our time, but it can also, ironically, be an obstacle to discovering our purpose.

You see, many of us were fed, along with our mother's milk, the idea that "you can be anything, do anything, have anything you want, sweetheart. . . . " All you have to do is watch the auditions for *American Idol* to see that this isn't true! While many people find that televised parade of humiliation entertaining, I find it painful to watch, because it reinforces for me the fact that people waste an awful lot of time trying to be something they are not, rather than being who they should be.

I see this all the time in young people I interact with. They have the freedom to do anything they choose, and yet they seem more purposeless and cynical than any generation that's come before. I meet new college graduates who are depressed about their lives, before they have even really begun venturing into the world. Sometimes too much choice can be a bad thing. The "freedom to be you and me" that the boomers passed on to their children has gotten way out of hand, and the result is a generation that is now dubbed "Generation Yawn." They have grown up getting everything they want, but have no sense of direction. The only way to start to find your way in the world is to take responsibility for the direction of your life. It takes focus and commitment to find and then develop and own that particular expression that you have to contribute to this world. There are three terms here that are critical: *develop, own,* and *contribute.*

I use the term *develop* because your creative expression might be something you are already doing, but only partially, or not in a way that is deeply fulfilling. So don't assume you have to abandon the career in real estate you've spent thirty years building so that you can take up pottery or learn the saxophone because that was the one thing you loved in school.

I know a real estate agent in Florida, which is currently one of the most depressed real estate markets in the country. She recently took up a practice of gratitude about her job that she shares with all her prospects, and her business is now doing better than ever. She says that by being grateful for whomever and whatever comes into her life each day, more people than ever are showing up. She's embodied an expression of gratefulness in her life's work and fulfills it through being a real estate agent.

When I say *own,* I mean embrace that expression so fully that it becomes the thing that unites your working life and your personal life, your financial life and your spiritual life.

And last, the term *contribute* points to a very important distinction. I think our uniqueness is found not in what has been *given to us,* by God or destiny or genetics, but in how we *contribute,* how we express ourselves in the world. Your unique expression could be found as a plumber, or a piano teacher, or the CEO of a multibillion-dollar corporation. It can be any job or activity where you find your joy and ultimately your sense of purpose in life. It's the expression of *who you are,* in the world.

In talking to thousands of people around the country, the ones who are successful—and by that I mean fulfilled and happy, as well as financially sustainable—seem to be the ones who found that same sense of purpose and expression for themselves. I'm talking about success at a level where you wake up every day excited about the prospect of what you're going to do. Sadly, I also meet a lot of people who are in jobs that they hate, or who remember having a sense that there was something they wanted to do but never found it. Those people don't wake up filled with joy.

One of the problems around all this is that we've been indoctrinated to compete. We've been taught that more is better. The school systems teach that; the grading systems teach that. Advertising and corporate America push the hell out of it—*more is better.* In this country, we've built a system where we try to convince everyone that the more money you make the happier you'll be. Interestingly, some studies have shown that that's not necessarily true. One study asked participants in four different income brackets to say whether they were "not too happy," "pretty happy," or "very happy." The percentage of people claiming to be "very happy" among those making less than $20,000 a year was only 22.2 percent, whereas in the group making $20,000–$50,000, the figure rose to 30.2 percent, and in the group making $50,000–

> **||||**
>
> **Our uniqueness is found not in what has been *given to us,* by God or destiny or genetics, but in how we *contribute,* how we express ourselves in the world.**
>
> **||||**

$90,000, it rose again to 41.9 percent. But interestingly, above $90,000, the percentage of people who were "very happy" barely changed, rising only 1 percent, no matter how high the income was. Those with the highest incomes were almost twice as likely to report being "very happy" as those with the lowest incomes, but there was very little difference above the $90,000 line. I guess we could conclude that money can buy happiness up to a certain point, but more money doesn't continue to buy more happiness.[4]

In my work as a financial planner, this conclusion has been backed up over and over again. Because I am one of the top producers in my company, I often get invited to speak to other financial planners about how to be more successful. They usually only invite me to speak to the top tier, those with six-figure incomes, so basically I often find myself sitting in a seminar room with a bunch of people who already make a lot of money and want to make even more. And I always tell them that making more money is not the point. This is not really what they are expecting to hear, so to get my message across, the question I always ask is: How many people remember thinking that if they could make $100,000 a year they would have everything they needed and everything they wanted? I ask them to think back fifteen or twenty years to that time when they were a new financial planner, perhaps making $15,000 a year, and thinking, "If I could just make $100,000 a year I would be happy, life would be smooth sailing, everything would be perfect." Without fail, every single person in the room will raise their hand and say they remember thinking something like that.

I hosted a radio show for a number of years called "Beyond Success: Redefining the Meaning of Prosperity." On that show, I talked to people all over the country who made millions of dollars a year, but many of them were still really miserable. I also talked to a lot of people who were unusually happy and successful, and what all those people had in common was not the amount of money they made. The thing they all shared was that they were each doing what they loved to do.

One of the happiest people I know makes about $30,000 a year. He is a ski instructor for handicapped children. He gets to ski all year round. When not skiing for his own pleasure, he gets the personal reward of teaching handicapped children a new skill.

For the past decade, social scientists and pollsters have been handing out complex questionnaires to hundreds of thousands of people around the world in an attempt to gather scientific data on what makes human beings happy. Two of the largest studies that rank the happiness of countries around the world are the World Map of Happiness from the University of Leicester and the World Database of Happiness from Ruut Veenhoven of Erasmus University Rotterdam. All the happiness surveys ask people basically the same question: *How happy are you?* ABC News even did a segment about the findings of these surveys, which were very revealing. The most striking thing that they found was that the happiest country on earth is not a tropical paradise. You probably haven't been there and would be unlikely to think of it as a holiday destination, let alone a place to live. It's not even warm. It's a cold, rather dreary little country tacked on to the top of Germany. It's Denmark. No offense to the Danes, but Denmark really doesn't seem like a contender for the "happiest place on earth."

So what's the secret of Denmark's success? Well, this is where it gets even stranger because the answer is higher taxes. Danes pay between 50 percent to 70 percent of their income to the government. Of course, there's a trade-off: The government covers the cost of all health care and education and spends more money on the elderly and the young than any other country in the world. But there's another unexpected effect of the high tax rates that may account for the Danes' happiness and may have something to teach us all. The tax rates have the effect of evening out the income discrepancies one would expect to find between, for example, a banker, a teacher, and a musician. A sanitation worker is paid as much as a doctor. And people don't judge each other's social status based on profession. Therefore, Danes are much more free to choose a career they love, one that makes them "hygge," as they say, rather than one that will bring them more money or status. So this speaks directly to the point I'm making: Unless you find what your unique expression is, what makes you happy in the world, you can't find true happiness.

By the way, the United States was way down on the happiness scale compared to Denmark.[5]

But before you make plans to sell up and move to Denmark, let me explain why the same principles can actually apply to your life right here and now, even though you may not live in such a supportive social structure. In my company, we have people who will come to work even when they're sick because they enjoy working here so much. At the end of the year, we have to force people to take their vacation time because they haven't taken it by year end. When you can create an environment where everyone wants to come to work, you see in those people a completely different sense of happiness and fulfillment than in a place where people don't. And it radiates.

SIGNPOSTS TO YOUR UNIQUE EXPRESSION

Most people will admit that they are their own worst enemy. We judge ourselves the most; we criticize ourselves the most. When all this self-criticism is going on in your mind, it's very difficult to show up in the world as the person you are supposed to be. Remember the meditation metaphor of the well with its layers and layers of sediment? The more you clear out those layers, the more the energy and light that is at the bottom of the well is exposed, so it begins to shine through you. And the more you let that light and energy shine through, the more you discover that's the real you.

The most important step in finding and eventually *owning* your unique expression is to begin your process of meditation. This is because your true unique expression doesn't come from your mind; it comes from a different place. You can call it whatever you want— the heart, God, your True Self. You can use my term "Source," if you like. But the point is that it's not going to come from you overthinking the process. It has to come from a more intuitive part of yourself, and in order to access that deeper place, you need to learn to disengage from your mind's endless chatter and let the light deep at the bottom of your well shine through. I strongly recommend that you not hurry to skip over the first pillar in your eagerness to find your unique expression; it's important also to approach the second pillar gradually and gently. As one of the world's greatest sages, Lao Tsu, wrote, back in the fifth century BC, "Do you have the patience to wait till your mud settles and the water is clear? Can you remain unmoving till the right action arises by itself?"[6]

Your true unique expression doesn't come from your mind; it comes from a different place.

While I don't necessarily expect you to sit on a meditation cushion and wait until your unique expression knocks at the door, I think this message of patience is essential. You may find that it takes some time to find out what you are supposed to be doing here, and in all likelihood, it will change and evolve over time. That being said, there are some simple ways you can begin to find and "own" your unique expression, by which I mean getting to that point where you are out in the world and making a living from your unique expression and not feeling any fear of scarcity.

When I was doing my radio show a couple of years ago, I interviewed many people who had a lot to say about success and happiness. I had the chance to talk to authors Dan Sullivan and Michael Ray about how to find your creative expression. Sullivan came up with four ways to know when you have discovered your creative expression. I liked his ideas so much I asked him if I could share them with you. According to Dan Sullivan:

1. The activity energizes you when you are doing it. (This is why I refer to your unique expression as a source of energy income.)

2. Other people say you're good at it. (I call this concept the *American Idol* test—and please, don't trust your friends or family to be objective. You have to find strangers who will say you're good.)

3. You can make a living at it. (I say more about this in a moment.)

4. You love to do it.

Michael Ray added some interesting pointers. He said that when a person finds her creative expression it feels intrinsically meaningful. It feels natural to do; it makes time go by quickly; you look forward to it; it makes you feel good about yourself. And the last and most important thing he added was that it is something that you feel contributes to the fulfillment of your purpose in life.

These observations echo the pioneering work of Dr. Mihaly Csikszentmihalyi, author of the best-selling *Flow: The Psychology of Optimal Experience*. Csikszentmihalyi defined and explored the concept of "flow"—as in "in the flow"—as an experience of optimal fulfillment and engagement. He described his life's work as the effort "to study what makes people truly happy." In the opening chapter of his book, he explains:

> In the course of my studies I tried to understand as exactly as possible how people felt when they most enjoyed themselves, and why. My first studies involved a few hundred "experts"—artists, athletes, musicians, chess masters, and surgeons—in other words, people who seemed to spend their time in precisely those activities they preferred. From their accounts of what it felt like to do what they were doing, I developed a theory of optimal experience based on the concept of *flow*—the state in which people are so involved in an activity that nothing else seems to matter; the experience itself is so enjoyable that people will do it even at great cost, for the sheer sake of doing it.[7]

Csikszentmihalyi was surprised by the similarities he found in people's experience across a diverse range of fields and activities. He identified some of the key characteristics of the state he calls *flow,* including a feeling of complete immersion in the activity (which echoes Michael Ray's observation that you forget about time in such moments). Other characteristics of flow are:

▌ A sense of being stretched but not overwhelmed

▌ A natural forgetting of all the things that bother people in everyday life

▌ A reduced awareness of the self as an entity separate from what is going on

▌ A feeling of being part of something greater

▌ An experience of being carried along with the logic of the activity

Csikszentmihalyi also sees the experience of *flow* as pointing to an evolutionary blessing that distinguishes human beings from all other species. In an interview with *What Is Enlightenment?* magazine, he said:

> My hunch is—and, of course, there is no proof of this—that if an organism, a species, learns to find a positive experience in doing something that stretches its ability; in other words, if you enjoy sticking your neck out and trying to operate at your best or even beyond your best, if you're lucky enough to get that combination, then you're more likely to learn new things, to become better at what you're doing, to invent new things, to discover new things. We seem to be a species that has been blessed by this kind of thirst for pushing the envelope. Most other species seem to be very content when their basic needs are taken care of and their homeostatic level has been restored. They have eaten; they can rest now. That's it. But in our nervous system, maybe by chance or at random, an association has been made between pleasure and challenge, or looking for new challenges.[8]

Another fascinating view on our evolutionary propensity for pushing the envelope came from twentieth century American psychologist Abraham Maslow, who is most well known for his theory of the hierarchy of human needs. Maslow, considered the father of Humanistic Psychology, observed that human needs are arranged in a hierarchy according to their degree of urgency. He famously represented these levels of need in a stratified pyramid, with the most basic needs at the bottom—the physiological needs for air, water, food, sleep, and sex. The next layer represents safety needs—security and stability—followed by a layer of psychological or social needs—for belonging, love, acceptance. Then come esteem needs, including the need for self-respect and recognition from others. In later versions, Maslow added cognitive needs and aesthetic needs to this level of the pyramid. (I even saw a posting on the Internet where someone added "iPhone needs" right under

Maslow's "esteem" level!) The top of the pyramid was what Maslow called the self-actualizing needs—the need to fulfill oneself.

The reason Maslow is so relevant to our discussion of success is that in sharp contrast to most of his forebearers and contemporaries in the field of psychology, he based his theory on healthy, creative people who used all their talents, potential, and capabilities, rather than on disturbed, neurotic, or mentally ill people. As he said, "If we want to answer the question, how tall can the human being grow, then obviously it is well to pick out the ones who are already tallest and study them."[9] This is one of the reasons that his ideas have been so popular in the business world, to the point where he is even hailed as the "father of modern management." His writings have been collected in *The Maslow Business Reader* and have inspired countless leadership books, programs, and courses. In his 2007 book *Peak: How Great Companies Get Their Mojo from Maslow,* visionary hotelier Chip Conley argues that "today's most successful companies consciously and unconsciously use Maslow's principle of human motivation every day."[10]

What is powerful about Maslow's observations is that he saw the drive toward self-actualization as a "need" in the same way that hunger is a need, but at a much higher level. As he put it, "Musicians must make music, artists must paint, poets must write if they are to be ultimately at peace with themselves. What human beings can be, they must be. . . . [Self-actualization] refers to man's desire for self-fulfillment, namely the tendency for him to become actually what he is potentially: to become everything one is capable of being."[11]

What Maslow's theory also made clear, however, was the idea that unfulfilled needs lower in the pyramid would inhibit a person from climbing to the next step. He gave the example that even someone dying of thirst quickly forgets his thirst when he has no oxygen. In the same way, someone whose safety is threatened has little concern for his reputation.

Maslow made a distinction between the lower levels of the pyramid, which he called "deficiency needs," and the level of self-actualization, which he described as a "being need." Csikszentmihalyi, whose observations came after Maslow's, saw these higher drives in the human psyche as being evolutionary by nature, because once they are fulfilled they do not simply die down, like hunger or the need for security, but motivate the individual toward higher levels of self-actualization. This is why he also called these levels "growth needs." He observed certain characteristics of people who seemed to have attained this level, noting that self-actualizing people tend to focus on problems outside of themselves, have a clear sense of what is true and what is false, are spontaneous and creative, and are not bound too strictly by social conventions. Self-actualizing people also tend to have many "peak experiences"—profound moments of love, understanding, or happiness, a sense of being that's more whole, more fully alive, both free or independent and yet connected to the whole world.

As you begin to explore your own creative potential, the insights of these thinkers can be helpful in illuminating the path forward. There is no set recipe for finding your unique expression, and as we will discuss more in the next chapter, it is something that evolves, and that you will play an active part in building.

Holocaust survivor Viktor Frankl once said, "Man should not ask what the meaning of his life is, but rather must recognize that it is he who is asked. In a word, each man is questioned by life; and he can only answer to life by answering for his own life." Don't wait for your creative expression to miraculously appear, or you may find yourself still waiting when you are on your deathbed. Use the insights of those who seem to have found "self-actualization" in their own lives to help you discover and begin to develop your own unique purpose in the world.

CHAPTER SEVEN

EXPRESSING YOURSELF

Your life has an inner purpose and an outer purpose. . . . Your inner purpose is to awaken. It is as simple as that. You share that purpose with every other person on the planet—because it is the purpose of humanity. Your inner purpose is an essential part of the purpose of the whole, the universe and its emerging intelligence. Your outer purpose can change over time. It varies greatly from person to person. Finding and living in alignment with the inner purpose is the foundation for fulfilling your outer purpose. It is the basis for true success.

—ECKHART TOLLE, *A New Earth*[1]

I BEGAN TO DISCOVER MY CREATIVE EXPRESSION WHEN I WAS selling insurance. This may not sound like a very romantic pastime, and it probably isn't the kind of thing that comes to mind when you think about "unique creative expression." But I actually loved that job, and I found in it the seeds that have blossomed into the life I am living today. Today I run a very successful financial services company that employs over thirty people. I'm also a personal coach, a seminar leader, a public speaker, and now an author. The story of how I moved from selling insurance to my present situation illustrates how a creative expression can evolve and develop, and how important it is to learn how to follow the signs and hang in there.

When I speak about finding and owning your unique expression, as covered in the last chapter, I'm not assuming that it is necessarily something other than what you are already doing. Granted, if you felt perfectly fulfilled and successful, you probably wouldn't be reading this book, so there are probably some changes you need to make. But you may not be as far from the track of your life's purpose as you think. When I coach people about this pillar, I always encourage them to start with the job they are in right now. Using the tools and exercises I will be sharing in this chapter, you can then find out if the seeds of your creative expression are right in front of you, at the desk you sit at every day. If you find that they are, I will show you how to make the changes necessary so that the job you've been dragging yourself to each day can blossom into a life that has you leaping out of bed in the morning. If not, I'll help you find out where your direction lies, and help you get started on your new journey.

IT *IS* ABOUT THE MONEY

Back to my favorite subject: money. You may wonder why I'm starting here, since the whole point is supposed to be about finding a greater fulfillment and purpose that lies beyond money and material possessions. But I think it's really important to start here for three reasons.

First, the fact is, in this world, you need money to survive. This brings us back to Maslow's hierarchy of needs. As explained in the previous chapter, the basic principle of Maslow's theory is the simple but powerful observation that our deepest motivations are ranked according to necessity, and if our most fundamental physiological and safety needs are not met, our attention will not move to the higher needs for social contact, esteem, and self-actualization. This is why your creative expression needs to make you money: If it doesn't, your attention is constantly going to be drawn down the pyramid to the more pressing issues of your survival and security, and it will be very difficult to find any lasting fulfillment even if you are doing the thing you love the most.

Second, there probably isn't going to be time for work *and* your unique expression, so your unique expression has to be your work. You have to find a way to get paid to do your unique expression, and it should be enough for you to survive on. While it might not make you fantastically rich, it's something that will give you so much joy doing it that as long as it can sustain you and support you, the idea of being rich might not be a need or desire anymore. For some people, their unique creative expression might be to become a priest or a nun, and serve the poor, like Mother Teresa did.

||||

You have to find a way to get paid to do your unique expression, and it should be enough for you to survive on.

||||

Those callings obviously won't make you a lot of money, but they sustain some people at such a deep level that they no longer feel the need for much more than the basic requirements for living.

The third reason money is so important is because it points to something deeper than your bank balance. While your creative expression doesn't need to make you fantastically rich, it needs to give you *what money represents to you*. It needs to satisfy your deepest core desires or values, and I've found, in talking to thousands of people across the United States, that asking yourself what money means to you is a very effective way of shining a light down into that well of your mind and looking straight at what shapes your personality and often defines your destiny.

Look at the blank page to your right and try to answer this question *in a single word:*

What does money mean to you?

You may remember that I pointed out earlier in the book that most people tend to define money in terms like "freedom," "power," or "security." In fact, those three words are the most common answers I hear, and I must have asked this question a thousand times. Perhaps your answer is different, but whatever it is, you can probably see that it falls into a similar category. My point is that when we are seeking money, on a deeper level we are seeking freedom, security, or power. Here's the key: Once we have freedom, or security, or power, we may find that we are less concerned with money, as long as we have enough to live comfortably on.

Pioneers of human nature have studied our desires, motivations, and values in great depth, and today psychologists, coaches, and even business consultants can help you to understand your personality type and how these underlying drives are impacting your financial success and personal relationships. One of the most insightful approaches is the work of Steven Reiss, a professor of psychology and psychiatry at Ohio State University, who spent five years developing and testing a new theory of human motivation based on the pioneering work of William James, which Reiss published in the book *Who Am I? The 16 Basic Desires That Motivate Our Action and Define Our Personalities.*

After conducting studies involving more than 6,000 people, Reiss concluded that sixteen basic desires guide nearly all meaningful behavior. Ranging from power and independence to honor and idealism to social contact, romance, and eating, these desires form particular combinations in each individual, which express themselves as personality traits. "These desires are what drive our everyday actions and make us who we are," he writes. "What makes individuals unique is the combination and ranking of these desires."[2]

For the purposes of this book, we don't need to get into the level of detail that includes our physical and social desires, but it is very important to understand some of the most fundamental desires that can influence our success. If you are interested in more fully understanding Reiss's sixteen core desires, I highly recommend his 2000 book *Who Am I?* or his 2008 book, *The Normal Personality.*

Let's take a closer look at the desires, motivations, or values that impact our success. Look back at the word you wrote on the previous page. Was it *freedom, security, power,* or something similar? Think about those three words. You probably feel like you want more than one of them—perhaps all three—but one of them pulls you more strongly. It's essential that your creative expression does not conflict with that overriding motive. It needs to satisfy your deepest, often unconscious desires in a healthy, socially acceptable way.

For example, if your passion is writing, but you have a strong desire for power, being the editor of a small local newspaper might not fulfill you. But how about being a scriptwriter for big-budget Hollywood movies? If your overriding concern is security and you love working with young people, the tenured life of a college professor would be much more fulfilling to you than a sports coach. If freedom is your desire, then focusing on a job that gives you control over your own time, like a computer consultant, author, or public speaker, would satisfy your desires more than a nine-to-five job.

These three desires are by no means the only ones that will impact your success, but in my experience they are the most fundamental. Once you are clear about these three desires, think about other things that matter to you. Perhaps idealism is a strong motivating force in your life. In that case you will need to make sure your creative expression is aligned with your sense of a greater purpose that fulfills your idealistic motives. Maybe you are a naturally curious person who loves to learn. If so, your creative expression will need to offer opportunities for growth and innovation so that you don't find yourself bored or frustrated.

When I got into the insurance business, I was drawn to it by two overriding desires: to be in control of my own destiny and to make a lot of money, which really added up to one thing: *freedom*. I had an uncle who was a very successful insurance salesman, and I could see that he had a lot of money; he worked three or four days a week, spent a lot of time with his family and at home pursuing his hobbies, and seemed really happy. My parents, in contrast, worked all the time and were really miserable. My father was laid off countless times. So that sense of freedom and happiness that my uncle had really pulled me toward a career in insurance early on.

‖‖

If we don't take into account our core values or desires, we are likely to find ourselves derailed, time and time again, without quite knowing why.

‖‖

Think about people in your life—family members, friends, colleagues—who seem to have what you want. Talk to them about what they do and how they got there, and find out what they love most about their job—what are the positive and negative aspects of it? Perhaps you have a friend who owns his own company and always seems to have a great deal of freedom and flexibility to spend time with his family or take a spontaneous afternoon off to play golf. He may tell you that he loves that freedom, but the downside is the sense of insecurity, the worry about whether he can break even this year. But it's worth it to him, and he wouldn't have it any other way. Then ask yourself: Could I live that way? Maybe freedom means that much to you, too.

But maybe security is a stronger value for you, and you would never be happy living with that degree of risk and uncertainty.

Asking these kinds of questions can help you get a sense of the hierarchy of your own values. And this is an important part of the process of finding and owning your unique creative expression. If we don't take into account our core values or desires, we are likely to find ourselves derailed, time and time again, without quite knowing why.

Have you ever been convinced that you want to achieve a certain goal, and yet you realize that you are continually shooting yourself in the foot? It could be because what you think you want to achieve is conflicting with a deeper desire that you are not conscious of. For example, you might be someone with a very strong desire to avoid power. Your job involves supervising a small group of people, and although you are efficient and good at what you do, you keep making silly mistakes that prevent you from being promoted. You might unconsciously be derailing your career development to avoid getting more responsibility and having to manage more people. As Robert Collier, one of the early self-help writers in the 1920s and 1930s, put it, "One might as well try to ride two horses moving in different directions as to try to maintain in equal force two opposing or contradictory sets of desires."

Knowing yourself at this level is an essential starting point for engaging with this pillar. Start with the job you are in, and ask yourself whether it satisfies your core desires or values. If it does, then it will give you confidence that you could already be headed in the right direction. If it doesn't, it may not mean you are completely on the wrong track, but you may need to take a new angle. For example, if your passion is music, but you have a strong desire for power, being a composer might not fulfill you in the long run. But how about being a conductor? As your unique expression starts to come into focus, keep referring back to this foundational question: Does my job satisfy my core desires?

IT'S NOT *JUST*
ABOUT THE MONEY

Finding your unique expression is often a very uncomfortable process, and I wouldn't be much help to you if I tried to pretend otherwise. It can be disconcerting and even frightening when you begin to disengage from the mind and from the unconscious drives and cultural assumptions that have been keeping you on a narrow track.

When you start listening to intelligence from another place, a deeper Source, it may at first be hard to hear and difficult to discern amid the tumult of your chattering mind. It can be disconcerting because sometimes that voice doesn't make a whole lot of logical sense and may not be in step with the way we've been taught to think for most of our lives. So you need to have a lot of patience with the process. It may take some time for the direction to come into focus, and there may be different threads within your current life that seem entirely disconnected but are destined to come together in unexpected ways. For this reason, I always encourage people to stay open to all possibilities, to take one step at a time and not draw any conclusions too quickly. Don't let your mind jump back in the driver's seat when things get too insecure.

I could never have predicted where my journey would take me. Although I got into the insurance business out of a desire for money and freedom, there were other desires that were also guiding me, intuitions of what was to become my unique expression. For example, in college, I had a sense of wanting to be a teacher, but I didn't want to teach people how to do math or physics; I wanted to teach them how to be happy and fulfilled. But I had no idea what that meant exactly. Public speaking was something I loved, and I had a great teacher who taught me how to do free flow seminars. I got an incredible amount of energy and joy from getting up in front of a group of people and doing a presentation and was always looking for that thing that I could teach that would make people happier. Meditation was the only thing that seemed to make me feel good and more connected. So back in 1990, I started teaching meditation while also giving seminars about insurance and other topics. I also started a speakers bureau, helping other people book seminars.

IIII

It may take some time for the direction to come into focus; you will need a lot of patience with the process.

IIII

And yet none of my efforts really amounted to anything. I was teaching and doing training seminars even though I hadn't reached financial success myself. But I knew instinctively at that point that it was not about the money. My wife was always asking me, "How long are you going to keep this up?" And I would say, "What do you mean? This is my career." My mother-in-law just kept leaving classified ads for jobs on our kitchen table.

One day, during the worst period financially, I sat down with a piece of paper and on the left side wrote everything I loved about what I was doing and on the right side, I wrote everything I didn't love about what I was doing. The left side of the paper had a lot of writing. I liked the people I worked with, I liked the flexibility in the hours, I liked the fact that I was constantly learning new things, and I liked the freedom. On the right side was one statement: "I'm not making enough money." That was it. I would look at that piece of paper frequently over that two-year period when I was really struggling and I knew instinctively that the lack of money wasn't a reason to give up what I loved doing. To trade what I loved doing for a job that I didn't love for more money was just not the right choice. I knew that eventually if I stuck it out doing what I loved, it would work out. So I kept telling my wife and mother-in-law that this was my career, and although it might take a while I was going to stick it out. I was committed. It fulfilled me. I never woke up once during that time of being broke and thought, "This isn't what I'm supposed to be doing," or "I don't want to go to work."

People sometimes seem surprised that I felt that passionately about being an insurance salesman. But it was a good living that also gave me the feeling that I was helping people, and it gave me a lot of freedom. I got to meet new people all the time—three or four different families every day. I loved that process, and it was in this opportunity that I eventually found another seed of my creative expression.

If you are in a difficult moment in your life, try the same exercise. Write down everything you love about your current job on one list and everything you don't like on the other. If you have more things on the right side of your list than the left, you may well be at a point where you need to make a big change. Some of the tools in this chapter can help you figure out what that is. If you have written down more things on the left than the right, hang in there. If the right-hand side of your page just says, "I don't make

EVERYTHING I LOVE ABOUT MY JOB	EVERYTHING I DON'T LIKE ABOUT MY JOB

enough money," hang in there. You can't ignore those things you don't like about your current job, and eventually your unique creative expression needs to answer them, but it may take time to get there. Keep that piece of paper somewhere close at hand and keep looking back at it—it will focus you on which areas you need to give attention to developing.

Most people put all their attention on what's not working. They worry about and focus on their lack of money. I learned to put my attention on what *was* working, and then invested more of my time and energy in that. I began to study investor psychology so that I could help clients make better decisions. I took communication courses to become more effective at leading seminars. And I participated in numerous personal development workshops in order to become more integrated as a human being.

IIII

Most people put all their attention on what's not working.

IIII

Try putting your attention on whatever aspects of your job you write on the left side of that piece of paper—the parts you love—and then expand your energy in those directions.

If you find nothing at all that you love about your job, then maybe the seeds of your unique expression will not be flowering there, and it is time to move on. Yes, even if you make a lot of money at that job! Try the following exercise as a way to find your sense of direction.

IF IT MAKES YOU HAPPY

If you are seeking the spark of your unique creative expression, whether within your current job or beyond it, take a tip from spiritual scholar Joseph Campbell and *follow your bliss.* You've probably heard that phrase plenty of times and thought "it sounds kind of nice, but I need some *direction.*" Well, I've turned "follow your bliss" into a practical thirty-day exercise that can give you a very clear sense of direction.

Don't worry—this is just a short process each night, but for it to be effective, you need to commit to it for thirty days. Each night before you go to sleep, reflect on your day. Scan through it, like a video recorder on fast-forward, and see if you can pause it on the most joyful, happy fifteen to thirty minutes. Write down in your journal what you were doing that led to that being the happiest part of your day. Were you riding a horse, working with children, playing piano, constructing a house? Was it a quiet moment with your sleeping child, or even a friendly debate with your creative team at work? Try to record all the details of exactly what you were involved in when you felt the best and happiest in your day's experience. Then the next night, do it again, without looking back at all. Turn the page and don't look back.

Once you find that pattern, that current of joy, it can point you to what you should be doing all day, every day.

Do this every night for thirty nights, and then put the journal away for two weeks and leave it alone. After two weeks, go back and read what you wrote, from beginning to end, and look for the connection between the thirty days. Is there a pattern that is easily visible? Was it every time you were working with children that you were happiest? Was it the thrill of taking risks, playing at the edge for the chance of a greater result? Was it when you were playing the piano? Was it in moments of creative engagement and teamwork? Once you find that pattern, that current of joy, it can point you to what you should be doing all day, every day.

For me, the happiest times of my day were found sitting with customers. I'd always had this feeling that I wanted to help people, and I discovered that by talking to them, even just in the process of selling insurance, I was making a difference. When I met with people, I made them feel better, and people always liked working with me. I had probably the highest sales ratio in the company even though I wasn't writing big enough policies to make a living. Pretty much everyone I met with bought something from me—but usually it was a very small insurance policy. So it really wasn't about the money—there was just something about the experience of meeting new people and making them feel good that fulfilled me deeply. It was that experience that made me want to be a financial planner, and I eventually gravitated toward that.

A LEAP OF FAITH

The next process, once you identify the happiest part of your day, is to look at ways you can eliminate what you do in the other parts of your day and let the best part of your day come forth more and more. For example, once I realized that just listening to clients and getting them to open up about their problems was the most joyful part of my day, I started looking at what I did with the rest of my time. I did a lot of paperwork and filling in applications. I had to call the home office a lot. I had to chase money that was coming in from other offices. That's how the insurance industry worked.

In the insurance world, there was an assumption that one person could do it all—you had to be the person who found the business, sold the business, did the paperwork, and took care of that business so it stayed on the books. You had to perform all four functions: They called them finder, binder, grinder, and minder. I knew that I was a really good binder and minder; I was really good at closing a dcal and keeping the business. But I was horrible at finding the clients and doing the paperwork: the finding and grinding.

I knew, because I understood my own strengths and weaknesses. Everyone has a unique expression, and you can create systems by bringing different people with different talents together to create a much better overall picture. By doing this in the insurance industry, I figured we could actually have more collective success, more happy people, and more sales. But none of the existing companies had that model in place. I had to create it myself.

So I developed a business plan and a marketing plan that would create the kind of organization I wanted to work in. It was quite radical at the time, because it was built around a model in which all four functions were different job titles. I planned to hire people to do those functions separately. To cut a long story short, I sold my business model to ING, which gave me the freedom to build the company I had envisioned. And from the very first day, I made a commitment to hire people, even if only part-time, who enjoyed doing the types of tasks that didn't bring me joy so that I would have more time to do what made me happiest. I loved going on appointments, but I hated cold-calling, and I hated paperwork. So I hired my sister to work part-time to do paperwork, and I hired two people to make sales calls.

Every six months I would review exactly what it was I was doing that I didn't love and how to get rid of it by having someone else do it. That's really how my business grew from one person to forty-five. I kept finding more and more ways to farm out what I didn't love to do to others who did enjoy doing those things so that I could do more and more of what I loved to do.

And it worked. I teamed up with people who enjoyed and excelled at the things I found tedious and frustrating. I only did the functions that I liked and excelled at. And the more I did that, the more successful we became together. It wasn't a win-lose situation—it was win-win.

The more I did what I loved to do, the more money I made, and the more everyone who worked for me was also happy and successful. So much so that in 2004, my employees nominated me as one of *Fortune Small Business* magazine's 15 Best Bosses in America—and I won. And I know that the reason they feel this way about me is because I honor each of their unique expressions. Everyone, from a secretary through to the top salesperson, feels valued. In my office, we don't try to put square pegs in round holes. As a business owner, it's important to me to match up a job description with someone who has the particular skills, talents, and modes of expression that meet that job. I want people to love what they do. When we do employee reviews, we support people in finding their creative expression, even if it means leaving us.

So my instinct to "follow my bliss" quickly proved itself. But there was a little bit of faith involved, too. In the beginning, I had to pay someone else to do the things I didn't like doing before I actually had the money to afford it. So I had to have faith that by freeing up the time to do more of what I loved to do, the money would quickly come in.

‖‖

If you can make a living doing work you don't enjoy, you can get much more out of life doing work that you love.

‖‖

Consistently, I found that it didn't take more than a few months to make up the income that I'd lost by paying somebody else to come in and do the job. But the willingness to take the initial risk was critical. One of the things that holds back many entrepreneurs is that they are unwilling to delegate any parts of their jobs; they are also reluctant to spend money that they don't have yet. That inability to take a leap of faith can be a major obstacle to success.

Following your bliss often seems like the harder, riskier route to take. We get comfortable in the known even though it doesn't bring us the joy we are looking for. But you have to believe that if you can make a living doing work you don't enjoy, you can get much more out of life doing work that you love.

YOUR CREATIVE EXPRESSION IS AN EVOLVING PROCESS

There is no one else like you. Through my particular line of work, I have met thousands of college professors and thousands of financial planners, and yet even in that narrow field, I can honestly say I've never met two people who are the same. However, what makes us unique is not just what we were born with. I believe our unique expression is a result of the particular confluence of personal talents, desires, life experiences, circumstances, and relationships that each one of us finds ourselves in.

To find your creative expression, you need to be sensitive to these different dimensions. For example, every financial planner, at his best, finds ways to relate with his clients on an individual basis. The different skills and talents that make up one human being are emphasized when that expression is intertwined with the needs of another human being. This is how your creative expression works in relationship to others.

Learn how to follow the threads of joy in your own experience. You may not know where one step will eventually lead you, or how those threads will come together to weave an integrated life. You may find as much insight by looking at the kinds of people you work best with as you do looking at yourself. It is essential to allow the time for your creative expression to evolve. Through meditation, cultivate the space in your mind to embrace tracks that may seem at first to be going in opposite directions, because eventually they may unite with a common purpose. What I'm saying boils down to this: Don't become fixed on any particular outcome. Find the seeds of your joy and then let them begin to grow; you may be surprised at what blossoms.

Remember how I said that back in college, I wanted to be a teacher? In fact, that was really how I saw myself, despite the fact that I was actually an insurance salesman. At one point, while I was still struggling to make enough money to live on, the company I was working for asked me to take part in a profiling program to help all of us salesmen find out what customer groups we worked best with. My profile said that working with educators was a good niche for me. And that made sense to me because that's kind of how I saw myself. Oddly enough, at the same time I had started marketing my speakers bureau to all sorts of groups in New Jersey. The groups I ended up working with the most were educational faculty associations. So I started providing seminars for free and quickly flowed into my niche market.

Working with educators is an important part of my creative expression, and had I not followed this particular thread in my own experience, I doubt I would have found quite the level of success and fulfillment that I did.

Another thread in my life that seemed connected to my deepest sense of fulfillment and joy was my love of public speaking and helping others through seminars. I always knew that I wanted to do some kind of motivational speaking. Back around 2001, I went to one of those Tony Robbins mega-motivational seminars. As I stood at the back of the huge crowd, watching as Robbins inspired and uplifted them, somehow I just knew beyond a shadow of a doubt that someday I, too, would be standing on a stage, speaking to thousands of people that same way. I had no idea how I was going to get there, but I thought to myself, "I'd better start practicing."

If you feel drawn to a kind of expression that seems completely outside of your current skill set and working environment, look for a way you can start to develop the skills and experience you would need to fulfill that role. Don't expect to be able to go from zero to sixty overnight—be prepared to work your way toward your goal. Just because something is part of your unique creative expression doesn't mean you are already good at it. You may need to invest in training, or you may need to be willing to volunteer your time in order to develop and learn.

My only platform for public speaking at that point in my life was financial seminars. Even when I reached a point where I was relatively successful, I didn't feel I had the stature or credibility to promote myself as a motivational speaker. So I started doing financial seminars across the college campuses in New Jersey. I didn't charge for these events—for me, they were an investment in my personal development. At times I was giving free seminars as often as once a week.

I loved public speaking, and doing the seminars gave me tremendous energy and joy. But that doesn't mean they were easy. In fact, there was a period of about a year when they were terrifying to me. It all began when I had to be rushed to the hospital one night with food poisoning. I almost died. You know that feeling of butterflies that you get right before you have to do something like public speaking? That was the feeling I had all night when I had food poisoning. So the next time I did a seminar and started feeling those butterflies in my stomach, I had a panic attack because it re-

‖‖

Look for a way to develop the skills and experience you need to fulfill roles you feel drawn to, even if they're outside your current skill set.

‖‖

minded me of having food poisoning. For almost an entire year I was doing a seminar every week, and every single time I had a huge panic attack—clammy hands, cold sweats, heart palpitations. I would stand up in front of the audience thinking I was going to black out or die. Yet I still had an intuitive sense that it was the right path, even though I was struggling so hard to do it.

It is important to remember that although your creative expression will be something you love, it may not always be easy. At times the process may be challenging, confusing, and even terrifying. At times like that, it's very important to hang onto those threads and not give up. Trust in the direction you are going, and don't be derailed because it doesn't always feel good in the short term.

One of the things that kept me going was that I was getting told all the time that I was doing a good job and that people loved my seminars. This goes back to the "American Idol test"—it's important to trust other people's feedback at times when it may conflict with your own experience. Don't be too proud to take criticism, either. If you consistently keep getting the message that you are not good at something, perhaps you need to rethink the way you are going about it. Let's say you have a strong desire to teach and help others and think you are supposed to be a motivational speaker, only you keep getting told that you have no presence or impact in front of a crowd. That doesn't mean your impulse to teach is wrong, but perhaps you are better suited to be a one-on-one coach. So listen to other people's impressions with an open mind and as much humility as you can muster.

In my case, I kept getting invited back to give more seminars, even though each time I stood up there I was thinking I must be doing a horrible job because I was ready to throw up and faint. But I kept accepting those invitations and just knew that I had to work through this fear and panic. The creative expression I was developing and the benefit that it was bringing to the people who came to my seminars was more important than my short-term personal comfort.

Hanging in there through all those seminars paid off for me, because they opened the door to a new platform for my creative expression. In 2004, Voice America, the largest online radio station, invited me to do a business radio show. I said I was interested, but that I was more interested in doing a show about success. It wasn't something I'd ever thought about doing before, but as soon as I got the call, it became clear to me that I should be doing a radio show about motivation and success.

However, once again, it didn't work out quite as smoothly as that. Voice America wanted a financial show, and they wouldn't accept my alternative proposal. I didn't really want to do a financial show, but I was hooked—a new sense of my creative expression was calling me, so I agreed to do what they wanted as long as they agreed that in six months they would review how I was doing, and if they liked me and my style, they would let me do a motivational and success show.

I quickly learned just how tough it was to meet compliance issues when doing a financial radio program. I would be on air, doing an interview, and the compliance people from ING would be calling me up in the middle of the show saying the guests couldn't be saying what they were saying about the market. It was a nightmare. After this happened a couple of times, they insisted that everything be prewritten before the show. I was horrified. How was I supposed to create an engaging and spontaneous show if I was reading everything word for word from a piece of paper? After a couple of months I got burned out. Despite my dreams of hosting a motivational show, I couldn't see doing it for all of six months. I called Voice America and said I couldn't continue with the show.

To my surprise, they said they really liked my style and my ratings were good, so if I wanted to, I could do the success show after all. So I started my show, "Beyond Success," and it was one of the most energizing, exciting things I'd ever done. For one hour, once a week, I would interview guests that I thought radiated success. I invited all sorts of interesting people to come on the show, and I learned more about success from doing that radio show than anything I'd done up to that point. I interviewed businesspeople, motivational coaches, spiritual teachers and activists, and purposely chose people who radiated happiness, fulfillment, and financial success while also making a real difference in the world.

The radio show gave me a very deep sense of fulfillment. It was the fullest expression of my own unique purpose that I had found, and it also taught me a lot about other people. I learned to observe whether someone was truly living their unique creative expression. I enjoyed reading the many books written by my guests, and was excited about the questions I would be asking them. And when they came on the show, I would look to see if the ideas were *alive* in them, whether they were "lit up," as I liked to put it, with the work they were doing. The energy either poured out of them or it didn't. It is critical that your expression in the world juices you up. I became convinced that you shouldn't be going to work only to be drained of your energy; you should be going to work and feeling the energy flowing through you. It was during those shows that this understanding of what it means to *earn energy* became a critical part of my success blueprint.

The radio show was a source of energy that began to overflow into other parts of my life. It was where the seeds of the Four Pillars were planted and nurtured, so that on that day in 2005, mentioned in Chapter 3, when I stepped onto the stage at that weekend business conference with no idea what I was going to say, a model of success that was integrated, practical, and spiritual suddenly blossomed right in front of my eyes and the eyes of the audience. That was the moment in my life when all the threads of my creative expression came together, when all the different melodies I had been playing merged into a symphony. My career as a salesperson, my development as a public speaker, my longing to teach, my financial planning expertise, my spiritual interests, and everything I had learned on the radio show all led up to that forty-five-minute talk. The unique creative expression that had been incubating inside of me for a very long time had its first real emergence.

But it didn't stop there. Remember, Maslow said that self-actualization needs only motivate further when they are fulfilled. I also began to do more motivational speaking, using the principles that had emerged at that conference in 2005. I would speak at libraries, colleges, wherever I could. And that experience naturally led to this book.

My coaching work took off at another level as well after that conference. A lot of people asked me for my number and card. I ended up coaching most of the people in that room in the weeks and months that followed. In those meetings, I found the ability to focus in on which of the Four Pillars someone was stuck in, then I could either guide them to a teacher or a book or a video specializing in one of the areas, or else personally get them to rework their own thinking.

I started to realize that I had a knack for this work—as long as I could get and stay out of my own way. If I could forget about myself and give all of my attention to the person I was speaking to or coaching, miraculous things seemed to happen. People would open up in ways they never had before. Some of them would start crying; emotional blocks would break down; problems and issues they had with money or their personal lives would naturally come to the surface. My financial planning clients started calling me their financial therapist. They were coming to our sessions more for counseling than financial planning. And the better I became at coaching and listening to them, the more I stayed out of the way, and the more my business grew as well.

GETTING OUT OF
YOUR OWN WAY

The notion of "getting out of the way" is not just a coaching technique. For me, it is paradoxically the whole point of self-actualization: the moment when you forget about the self altogether. That's always been the goal of spiritual practice in many traditions, especially those that come to us from the East—self-transcendence or ego-death. But many of us who have grown up in secular Western traditions have a hard time with this idea, because we've spent our whole lives trying to develop the self, heal the self, improve the self, and fulfill the self.

What I love about the idea of a unique creative expression is that it embraces both self-fulfillment and self-transcendence. In this sense, it unifies business and spirituality. It brings fulfillment to the self and develops the self, but at the same time avoids the danger of becoming overly self-focused, because it encourages us to focus our expression outward to the extent that we forget about ourselves. Maslow discovered the same thing when he was exploring self-actualization. He wrote:

> . . . [S]elf-actualization work transcends the self without trying to, and achieves the kind of loss of self-awareness and self-consciousness that the easterners . . . keep on trying to attain. [It] is simultaneously a seeking and fulfilling of the self *and* also an achievement of the selflessness which is the ultimate expression of the *real* self. [This work] resolves the dichotomy between selfish and unselfish. Also between inner and outer . . . the inner and the outer world fuse and become one and the same.[3]

That, to me, is spirituality—when the inner and outer fuse into one expression. Too often, the idea of spirituality becomes reduced to following a certain set of dictums or principles, or it goes to the other extreme and places no value on anything other than subjective emotional states. But we don't think of a person as "spiritual" because of how that person tells us he or she feels, nor do we think people spiritual because of the principles they proclaim. We call someone a spiritual man or woman because of the way that individual has lived this life. We seem to instinctively know that it is when our *expression* in life leaves the world a better place that the term *spiritual* is deserved. So that, to me, is what both spirituality and business are all about: following my life's purpose and expressing that purpose in the world.

‖‖‖

We consider someone spiritual because of the way that individual has lived this life.

‖‖‖

Recently, I was visiting a spiritual center here in the United States, and in the men's room, on the wall above the sinks, there was a framed quote from the jazz legend John Coltrane. I wanted to write it down and take it home with me, but I had no pen. So I took a picture of it with my cell phone. I loved this quote so much that it has stayed with me. It says:

> My goal is to live the truly religious life, and express it in my music. If you live it, when you play there's no problem because the music is part of the whole thing. To be a musician is really something. It goes very, very deep. My music is the spiritual expression of what I am—my faith, my knowledge, my being.[4]

That quote is a perfect expression of what Owning Your Unique Expression is all about. It's about being a force for good in the way that only you can be. And it's about being integrated, being whole, finding ways to spend the majority of your time to bring together, in one place, all the different aspects of who you are. It's about expressing yourself in a way that comes from the very Source of who we all are and flows out freely into the world around you. Finding and owning your own unique expression is what you are here on earth to do.

Remember, finding and owning your unique creative expression is not a fixed or static goal. It is a process that evolves through time, and it may look very different over a number of years. As you practice Connecting to Source and clear away more and more of the silt that obscures your true self, you will get a clearer sense of how you can express that Source in the world. But there's nothing to wait for—you can start right now, in the job you are doing, and begin the evolutionary process of owning your unique creative expression. Just listen carefully for that intuitive voice, and don't worry if at first it seems to contradict itself.

IIII

Finding and owning your unique creative expression is a process that evolves through time, and may look different over a number of years.

IIII

So many people are looking in the wrong direction, looking to the outside world to show them what they should be doing and to provide them with the energy to do it. Start right where you are and look within. The most critical thing in life for any human being is to know what they want to be *doing*. If your goal is "to be happy by achieving x, y, or z," you will find yourself frustrated and dissatisfied. But when you start focusing on what you want to express and contribute, you will discover a source of limitless energy and inspiration. The people I've met who I would describe as happy are all people who are so focused on what they are doing that they don't have time to even think about whether they are happy or not. They are simply driven by an overwhelming need to express themselves and to contribute to the world.

Go as deep into your own self as you can. Practice the first pillar, Connecting to Source, and let the light shine through from the bottom of the well. Look for the current of joy that is guiding you to the way in which you are supposed to express that light. When you begin to align yourself with your unique creative expression, your energy will flow from within, released by the activity itself, and you will see its effects all around you.

THE
THIRD
PILLAR

REDIRECTING
YOUR ATTENTION

**The empires of the future are the
empires of the mind**
—*SIR WINSTON CHURCHILL*

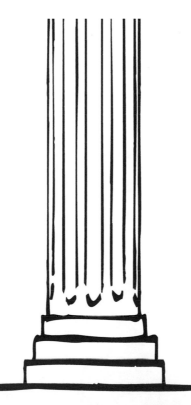

CHAPTER EIGHT

INVESTING IN A FUTURE YOU

Let the future tell the truth and evaluate each one according to his work and accomplishments. The present is theirs; the future, for which I have really worked, is mine.

—*NIKOLA TESLA*

I CAN'T TELL YOU HOW MANY PEOPLE I MEET WHO ARE MAKING a sizable income, have a family they love and care for, and yet are making no provisions for their future. In my practice, the percentage saved for retirement goes down as people make more money, not up as you might expect. It almost seems that as we make more money we become more convinced that buying more things will make us happier. If I could boil financial planning down to one sentence, it would go something like this: "If you don't invest anything for retirement, you can guarantee it will be pretty miserable." Like most pieces of good financial advice, that sounds pretty simple, obvious, and sensible, but it can be surprisingly difficult to get people to put it into practice.

The third pillar gives you similar advice for your attention. It teaches you to invest in who you want to be in the future. The basic principle is that if you don't invest attention in your future, when you arrive there you will have no energy to be who you are hoping to be. If you spend all of your attention worrying about the past and the present, don't be surprised if the future doesn't look like you hope it will.

Practicing the third pillar, as I'll explain, only asks for five or ten minutes of your time and attention each night. It's a small price to pay for showing up in the future at a destination you have chosen. And you get a surprisingly large return on your investment. What you will discover when you begin to consciously devote attention to the future is that your energy seems to grow exponentially in the present moment, giving you the fuel to create the future that you desire. It's a bit like earning interest on your investment. Einstein famously said that "compound interest is the eighth natural wonder of the world and the most powerful thing I have ever encountered," and that statement seems even more true, in my view, when the currency is attention.

BACK TO THE FUTURE

Often, when I'm training salespeople, I'll ask, "What are you going to do different this year than you did last year?" And people always give me a kind of blank look. They come in with their goals: "I'm going to make more money than I did last year." "I'm going to see more people than I did last year." But when I ask them what they will do differently than last year, they say, "What do you mean?"

A well-known definition of insanity is doing the same thing over and over again and expecting different results. And when I talk about doing the same thing, I mean at the most fundamental level—how we spend our attention and energy. If we are living our lives with our attention endlessly caught up on the gerbil wheel of the same old thoughts, it's no wonder our lives don't change—even if we attempt to change our outward circumstances. By the time we get around to changing circumstances, it is already too late. Our energy and attention has already created the outcome we are experiencing in the present moment. But if we can get down to the level of where we spend our attention and begin to *redirect* it, we can begin to create a new destination for our lives. When we start being choosy about the thoughts we give our attention to, many people are amazed at how quickly and easily we can get what we want.

Redirecting your attention is about a change of orientation. It's a shift from the past and the present to the future. You may think you want the future to be different, but if you look honestly at your own experience, you will probably find that you don't give the future much attention. Our attention tends to gravitate first and foremost to how we feel in the present moment. We notice that we don't feel good, and we try to do something about it. But what we don't realize is that *the present moment has already happened*. What I mean by this is that the present moment is a result of our past choices, of the way we've spent our energy and attention in every moment leading up to it. The only way to really change the present would be to go back and change the past.

Pretty much everyone I know has seen the classic movie *Back to the Future*. In case you are one of the few who missed it, here's a brief recap: In 1985, skateboarding teenager Marty McFly (Michael J. Fox) accidentally travels back to the year 1955 in a plutonium-powered time machine invented by his mad-scientist friend Doc Brown. Landing in the high school where his parents were teenagers, Marty unknowingly interferes with their first meeting and finds himself having to play matchmaker to ensure that he has a future to go back to. In a memorable scene, at the dance where his geeky father and his pretty, popular mother were supposed to have the kiss that began their improbable romance, Marty pleads with the band not to cancel their gig after the guitar player gets his finger slammed in the trunk of the car.

"Wait, you don't understand," he begs. "If you don't play, there's no music. If there's no music, they don't dance. If they don't dance, they don't kiss and fall in love and I'm history." In the end, he jumps onstage himself and lets rip with a guitar solo that leaves the crowd in shock. ("I guess you guys aren't ready for that yet," he says. "But your kids are gonna love it.") After many near misses, his parents finally kiss, and Marty's future is assured. Along the way he also takes care of his dad's low self-esteem and his mother's alcohol problem, thereby creating himself a much better future than the one he left behind.

▌▌▌

How concerned are you with trying to feel better about your past, in the hope that it will change how you feel about your present?

▌▌▌

Watching that movie today, most of us would probably see it as entertaining, if rather dated, science fiction. But we probably don't realize that we ourselves are engaging in that kind of science fiction with our own minds every day. How much time do you spend thinking about the past, wondering how things would be different "if I just had done this or that." How concerned are you with trying to feel better about your past, in the hope that it will change how you feel about your present? If you've been to therapy, this is basically what therapy sessions come down to. Now, I have nothing against therapy, and I know it can be very helpful to many people in many ways, but the one thing it can't do is change the past, no matter how much we dig in there and talk about it, process it, release our feelings about it. We may feel better about the past, but it is still the past, and the present is still the past too, from a certain point of view. It's already out of our control. So it's important to question how much of your precious attention is worth spending on yesterday—or today, which is yesterday's already inevitable result.

As a financial adviser, I would stake my reputation on the fact that the most important investment you can ever make is the investment of your energy and attention—the currency of success—in your own future. You will be surprised at what becomes possible when you begin to consciously direct your thoughts toward the future you want to create.

You may be wondering whether this advice doesn't contradict the first pillar, which is all about stepping out of the stream of thoughts in your head and letting those thoughts go by without getting caught up in the stream. Now we're talking about using thought to create our future. But the two concepts don't conflict—they're just different parts of the same process. Connecting to Source is essential for learning how to stop being tossed about by the stream of thoughts, without a life vest. Now in this third pillar, we're reclaiming our right to direct ourselves within that stream. We're getting back in the stream in a rowboat with two oars and steering our way in the direction we want to go.

Having a direction is essential. A lot of spiritual teachers will tell you that if you just let go of your thoughts and learn to be in the present moment, everything will take care of itself. But I've not found this to be the case. In the words of the inimitable Yogi Berra, "If you don't know where you're going, you'll wind up somewhere else." To me, getting out of the thought stream is what creates the space to take control of my life and direct it where I want to go. It's what releases the creativity that brings me the greatest joy. So I'm not a great believer in the present moment, because the present has already happened. I let go of my attachment to the past so that I can consciously build my future.

A LIFE-CHANGING
CUP OF COFFEE

I learned this simple principle about a decade ago, and it has transformed my life beyond recognition. I remember when I first discovered how much of my attention was unconsciously focused on my past. It was back at that time when I was an insurance salesman, trying to support a wife and a new baby and a mortgage on less than $20,000 a year. Those were the days when my mother-in-law used to leave classified ads on the kitchen table. Tucked away in my pocket was that piece of paper where I had written down everything I loved about my job on one side, and on the other side, that single sentence: *I'm not making enough money*. I was determined not to quit, but I couldn't see my way out of the financial quagmire I was getting sucked into deeper by the day.

One day I met up with a friend who had been studying neuro-linguistic programming (NLP). That may sound like some rather unpleasant form of brainwashing, but it is actually quite a powerful system for understanding how patterns in the brain interact to create our subjective reality and influence our behaviors. NLP practitioners take their cues from body language, and particularly from the movement of the eyes, to detect these patterns.

Over coffee at the local diner, I was telling this friend about my childhood, remembering my dad and how tough and strict he was, how he constantly put me down and made me feel like a failure. Over the rim of his coffee cup, my friend's eyes narrowed, focusing in on my own as I was speaking.

Unexpectedly, he said, "Imagine yourself at your senior prom." Surprised but intrigued, I did as he asked. That memory wasn't hard to conjure up—the powder blue tuxedo, my mullet haircut, and Def Leppard playing as we slow-danced the night away. Then he said, "Imagine yourself driving your first car when you got your license." I smiled as the image of that bright red Plymouth Scamp bobbed to the surface of my mind, recalling how my friends used to get out and run up most of the hills that my car could barely climb.

"Now imagine yourself with your father. He's yelling at you." That one wasn't hard, either. My father would take any opportunity, it seemed, to criticize me, especially when I was trying really hard. Like the first shooting competition I was ever a part of back in 1978. Images of that day came flooding back to me: the piercing blue of the sky, the sound of gunshots, those three perfect bull's-eyes, my father's stern voice telling me I must hit the last two perfectly . . . and how he yelled at me and then didn't speak to me for a week after I managed to completely miss both targets.

Abruptly, my friend broke eye contact, put down his coffee cup, and concluded the five-minute conversation that would change the course of my life. "All the images of your past are stored in your past, where they belong," he said, "except the last one. The image of your father yelling at you as a child is framed in your future."

In that instant, my life made sense to me. I had always thought I wanted to succeed. But actually I had spent fifteen years being average because all of my attention was focused on that past image of myself that was shaped by my father's constant criticism. I couldn't stop his criticism, no matter how hard I tried, and it was at those times when I tried the hardest that the emotional impact was most crushing. So I discovered early on that it hurt less if I didn't make the effort in the first place. Not trying became my shield, and as the years went by, my childhood defense had become my adult prison. No wonder I was miserable and felt like a failure. As Abraham Maslow wrote, "If you deliberately plan on being less than you are capable of being, then I warn you that you'll be unhappy for the rest of your life."[1]

From that day on, I began striving. My attention was freed from the past and began to be guided by the image of my own higher potential—my strengths, my desires, my dreams. I started reading more, and the book that really caught my attention was called *Advanced Psycho Cybernetics and Psychofeedback* by Paul Thomas. Not exactly a snappy title, but that book was pivotal for me. It explained that the human mind is a biocomputer that has input and output. Basically it said that whatever you put in you get out. If you put in junk, you get junk as an output. If you put in good programs, you get good results. His ideas made a lot of sense to me, so I started a program of creative visualization that was recommended in the book.

The process was very simple. I made a little "movie" in my mind that showed me having everything I wanted to have in five years' time. I played that movie to myself every night before I went to sleep. I visualized that in five years I would be living in a big house on two acres with acres and acres of woods behind me. I would be driving an Infiniti. I would be obviously out of debt; I would have my own business in a beautiful office building with twenty people working for me, seeing college professors all day and enjoying talking to them about life, helping them with their goals and their dreams. That was 1997. In 1999, I bought my house on two acres of land with a 160-acre tree farm behind it. By then, I was driving an Infiniti Q45. In April 2000, I started Gitterman & Sacks, setting up business in a huge office building with about 5,000 square feet of office space and with five employees, which has grown to forty-five employees since then. My company was managing millions of dollars in assets, and I doubled my income every year since 1997. Within less than three years, I had everything I had put in my movie.

Now, there's a lot more to my personal journey than this everything-I-ever-wanted success story ending. That was really just the beginning. But it's a very important part of my story because it proves that these methods *work*. They get results. If you have a clear destination and redirect your attention consistently toward it, you will get there—probably quicker than you expect. For me, what lay beyond success was a fulfillment brought about by teaching others how to connect to something deeper in life that would ultimately flower as their unique expression. For you, it could be working with children, trying to create a more sustainable environment, or getting involved in politics. Often, the problems that most affront us provide us with the direction in which to go. But if you don't have a clear direction, I can all but guarantee you won't get very far at all. As Zig Ziglar said, "If you aim at nothing, you'll hit it every time."

IIII

If you have a clear destination and redirect your attention consistently toward it, you will get there.

IIII

A metaphor I like to use comes from one of the fruits of my success: my car with its built-in navigation system. If your car doesn't have one, you've probably been in a car that does. When I get in that car, I enter my destination, the place I want to get to. For example, if I want to go to the city to meet a new client, I enter the address and the system guides me along on my journey— turn right, turn left, drive straight ahead for three miles.

Soon—within ten years, my friends at Intel tell me—I'll probably be able to get in my car, type in the address, sit back and read a book while the car automatically takes me exactly where I want to go. For now, I still have to drive it. But my car is pretty smart. It has a camera beside the rearview mirror that looks out at the road in front and sets off a warning system the second the car starts to change lanes without me having put my blinker on. It also has a radar detector so that when I set the cruise control and I get within 150 feet of the car in front of me, or a wall, or an embankment, the car automatically slows down.

So my car can do almost everything that I can do. But there is one crucial thing it's missing: I have no program in my car saying where I want to go and where I need to get to. I still have to tell it where to go—I have to program the navigation system with a destination. But imagine if I got into my car, thinking I wanted to go to the city, but because of some subconscious issues connected to my past, I entered the address of somewhere I went yesterday, or last week. I'd be driving in circles.

In a way, our subconscious mind is a bit like a navigation system. We're constantly being given directions by our subconscious mind, but if we haven't plugged in the right address with our conscious mind, if we haven't set that destination, then our subconscious mind is constantly going to lead us around in circles. As long as my attention was programmed with that negative self-image from my past, it was impossible for me to really create the future I thought I wanted.

||||

Our subconscious mind is a bit like a navigation system: If we haven't set the destination, it's going to lead us around in circles.

||||

Everything that the mind tends to say when we are not controlling it is negative feedback. Have you ever heard your mind say "you're the most wonderful person in the world, you're great at everything, I love you"?

Think about how you view yourself in your own head. Do you think mostly about the things you feel you're lacking—do you think you're not pretty enough, smart enough, articulate enough? Do you spend most of your time dwelling on the things that hold you back? This is how the unconscious mind keeps its grip on us. The mind has a fear of fulfillment, and as a perfection-seeking organism its job is to keep telling you what's wrong, what you can keep striving for. It thrives on the negative dialogue, and the more engaged with life you become the less attention you will end up giving it.

Look at how much of your day is accomplished by your unconscious rather than your conscious mind. Countless physiological processes continue more or less perfectly, without you having to think about them. Imagine if you had to remind yourself to breathe, or tell your kidneys to flush out impurities, or instruct your heart to pump blood 108,000 times a day! Your unconscious biological mechanisms accomplish all of these functions, leaving your consciousness free to take care of all the things you need to think about.

| | | |

The present is the result of the past.

| | | |

An analogy I use is that the conscious mind is like the captain of a ship, while the unconscious mind is the ship. Much of the ship is submerged in the water, and the captain has to stay on the bridge, never going inside the engine room or even knowing everything that is going on below decks. But he has a very important job: to set the course for the ship to follow. In the same way, the conscious mind can set a course for the unconscious mind to follow.

That's what entering a destination address into your navigation system does: It sets a course. The moment I reprogrammed my inner navigation system, I began moving forward at a pace that stunned those who knew me. Within three years, I was the top salesperson in the company, successful beyond what I could have imagined possible. All it took was that shift of attention, and then the readiness to change.

It may seem like we're heading into esoteric territory when we start talking about how our thoughts create our future. But it's not really that mystical when you think about it. The present is the result of the past. It's not any mystical conversation, it's a logical deduction.

MOVING FROM AUDIENCE MEMBER TO DIRECTOR

The metaphor of a movie is good for understanding the third pillar. Somewhere at the back of that movie theater, there is light shining through film and projecting that image onto the screen you are watching. Let's say that the projector represents your attention. The film is what you choose to put your attention on—those thoughts, self-images, desires, or dreams that you are focusing on. The light coming through the projector is the light of Source, and the screen it projects onto is your life. Using this simple metaphor, you can find out a lot about yourself. What movie are you playing? And where are you in it? Are you an actor on that screen, consciously playing out your chosen life? Or are you sitting in the audience, shouting helplessly at the screen?

The point is, if you are sitting in the audience, you're actually in the past. By the time that image hits the screen, it's already been scripted. Most of us relate to our lives this way—feeling that somehow we have no control over where we have ended up. We feel like audience members watching our own lives, victims of circumstance and our own unconscious drives. So the first step we have to take before we can take responsibility for our future is to take full responsibility for our present.

You have to accept as an absolute fact that you have created the life that you are living. Any idea, any notion, any belief you are holding onto that says someone or something outside of you is responsible for the life you are living today—a bad parent, those kids who bullied you at school, the dot.com crash that caused you to lose all your money, the business partner who ripped you off, even someone who committed a horrible crime against you, even the terrible tragedy that killed the love of your life—that is what is keeping you stuck where you are.

I'm not discounting the impact of those people or events, and I'm not saying that what they did was your fault. This is not about assigning or reassigning blame—it's about reclaiming control of our freedom to choose. We've all been victims, at one time or another, but the point is, we can either let that victimhood become our identity, or we can choose not to. As long as we see ourselves as victims, we disempower ourselves. We don't have to deny our past, but we can take responsibility for our present.

The third pillar asks you to simply suspend disbelief for a short period of time each day. I'm not suggesting that you have to go through your day saying positive things to yourself like the classic self-help books used to tell us. That doesn't work—because it doesn't take into account that the present has already happened. And I'm not saying you have to change the thoughts that are going through your mind, because technically that's not possible. What I'm saying is that you can choose what you pay attention to in your mind. And over time, if you have a vision, which is what that little movie I played to myself represented, you can start to retrain your attention away from the habitual downward spiral of thoughts. It doesn't stop the negative thoughts; they're still there. But the visualization process redirects your attention onto something else. Directing a movie in your mind gives you something to put your attention on that isn't the same old pattern.

I can't stress enough how important this is: If you don't take on full faith that you are creating the life that you are living, that you are the principal author of your own destiny, that you are writing your own story every day, you will remain a helpless audience member watching your own life go by, and neither I nor anyone else will be able to help you. You may get emotionally caught up in the plot line, and feel bad for the downtrodden hero, or angry at those who abuse and betray him. Your emotions react to each scene but you have no control over what is playing out on the screen.

However, if you are willing to accept responsibility for the role you have played and are playing in your life, you will become an actor rather than an audience member. Whatever you are doing now is the script you've been handed. So your responsibility is to be the best expression of that role you can be—to take full responsibility for it and not blame anyone else. Once you start doing that, everything changes—sometimes instantly. The victim mentality is what keeps you embedded in your present movie.

If you don't take on full faith that you are creating the life you are living, and you are the principal author of your own destiny, you will remain a helpless audience member watching your own life go by.

But this third pillar can actually take you further—from audience member to actor to director of your life. The director of a movie knows that each character is an integral part of the larger story. He has a broader goal: to have an impact on the world through making the best possible film that he can. A good director is fully in control of his creation, but he can only hope that his message and expression is well received. He can't agonize over that—he must have all his attention on the movie he is creating, on the actors, the crew, and all of the hundreds of people who are participating in his vision. His attention is glued to the present moment—that's how he is creating his future. Remember, *the future is the only thing we have any control over*. We can't change the past and we can't change the present, but what we can do is live life *now* in a way that will create the future we want. So let's get you a director's chair and a megaphone and start making your movie.

CHAPTER NINE

SUCCESS IS A JOURNEY, NOT A DESTINATION

Your future hasn't been written yet.
No one's has. Your future is whatever you
make it. So make it a good one. . . .

—*"DOC BROWN," Back to the Future III*

VISUALIZING THE FUTURE IS A VERY SIMPLE EXERCISE. HERE'S how it works: You create a two-minute video in your mind of you in the future, being the person that you always wanted to be, if only you had enough money to start. Imagine that money is no longer an obstacle—anything is possible.

This process requires just five minutes a night, before you go to bed. First, spend a minute or two meditating or doing some kind of relaxation technique. There's one that I like which is as simple as tensing and relaxing each muscle. Lie in bed with your eyes closed. Then tense your ankles, then relax your ankles. Tense your calves; relax your calves. Tense your thighs; relax your thighs. As you do this exercise, say to yourself, in your head, "I'm tensing my ankles; I'm relaxing my ankles. I'm tensing my calves; I'm relaxing my calves." Go right on up your body: thighs, stomach muscles, arms, neck. When you get to your face, tense and then relax your eyebrows and your lips. Don't rush through it. Once you've gone through that process, play your movie in your head. And your movie has to be of you playing bigger in the world.

When I say "playing bigger" in the world, I mean you should picture yourself living your unique expression to the fullest. Let's say, for example, that you're a plumber, your movie might be about having your own business. So you're going to imagine what a day in the life of you would look like if you were doing whatever it is that brings you joy. Maybe it would be working as a plumber in a nonprofit school for kids. Or maybe you're a school teacher and you want to be school teacher of the year. Perhaps you want to be creating programs, not just teaching other people's programs. So then your movie would show you teaching your own programs and affecting the lives of children in a way you are not doing now— reaching them in the way that deep down you know you can reach them. And kids would come up to you after class and say, "This is the best class ever; you're my favorite teacher." No matter how successful you already are, there is always a higher level you can envision. Think about Bill Gates—he's one of the most successful people in the world, but his goal is now to put a computer in every child's hands. Or U2 singer Bono, who is not just enjoying being the leader of one of the most famous rock bands in the world, but has dedicated himself to ending poverty in Africa.

The most important thing is that you are doing what you love. It doesn't necessarily mean you have to be an entrepreneur or strike out on your own. There are plenty of people who love what they do working for someone else. Some of my employees will come to work even if they're sick because they love being here. So in your movie you might be working for someone with whom you have a great working relationship; you don't have the risk and responsibility of owning your own business, and you get to express what you love doing in a comfortable, happy environment.

Sometimes people ask me, "Can I visualize being married to so-

and-so?" or "Can I visualize my estranged father finally speaking to me again?" And I always say no. This is because the power of attention gives us the ability to change our own future, but not to control other people. Of course, you hope your future will include all those you love, and it probably will. But for the purposes of this exercise, keep your focus on yourself. This also helps avoid a common pitfall: too often, what tends to happen when we in-

Your movie is just a snapshot of a day in the life of you.

clude other people in our movie is that we quickly start focusing on what *they* need to change, rather than what we need to change ourselves.

Your movie is just a snapshot of a day in the life of you. Try to go from morning to night and make it as sensory as possible, so you can see the house you want to wake up in, and you can smell the air when you walk outside. In his book *Advanced Psycho Cybernetics and Psychofeedback,* Paul G. Thomas explains why this is important:

> There are two ways that a person is able to use his imagination: *objectively* and *subjectively.* When people use their imaginations objectively, it is as though they were looking at a screen and see-ing a moving picture. They can "see" themselves doing some-thing, but they do not really feel that they are participating in the action. For example, as I am writing this . . . I can imagine putting down my pen, pushing the chair back, standing up, walking through the French doors, stepping onto the concrete pathway, walking the ten or twelve feet of concrete past the lemon tree. . . . I imagined that, but I did it objectively. I was completely removed from the experience.
>
> With a little more effort, I could have imagined the same thing subjectively. I could actually have felt and *experienced* the same things I was imagining. . . .[1]

Try to add as much detail to your vision as you can—objectively and subjectively. What car do you drive to work? And then what do you do when you get there? Whatever it is, it should be you living your fullest expression and being filled with happiness doing what you love to do. It's as simple as that.

It's important to allow room for your movie to evolve. Don't think of it as some ultimate end goal, the pinnacle of your success and perfect happiness. Think of it as a reachable first base. You may find that a whole different path opens up to you that you can't yet foresee, but for now, it's easiest to start by taking what you are already doing and just imagining yourself doing it in a bigger way that allows you to focus on what you love.

I always tell people not to tie their movie too closely to a financial goal. Why? Because your subconscious mind, the way I understand it, can only work on images of what you're expressing or doing in the world. It can see you driving a new car, but if you try to imagine a dollar or a million dollars in your mind, it's just a pile of green stuff. It doesn't mean anything to your subconscious. It's not an address that you can put into your navigation system. An address needs to be a clear visual picture of what you look like in the world—what you have, what you are expressing—and actual money just doesn't have any part in it. Your subconscious can grasp a million different expressions of *you* acting in the world in a unique way—doing motivational seminars, being a successful painter with your own studio, for example—but it doesn't get the concept of a dollar. I've seen people try it a thousand times; it doesn't work. So the movie has to literally be about you having as much joy as possible doing what you love to do, which takes into account that money is no longer an obstacle.

You need to play your movie every night for thirty days, because this is how long I believe it takes for a new habit to form in the subconscious mind. For example, if you smoke once, maybe it doesn't become a habit, but if you smoke for thirty days you're hooked. So you need to play your movie for thirty nights before you go to bed, until your subconscious gets hooked on your future image.

Then—and this can be the hardest part—you have to suspend all doubt and all negative influences. Most people, as soon as they imagine something bigger for themselves, immediately turn their attention to all the obstacles they think their mind needs to work through and come up with countless reasons why the process won't work before they can get to it. So you have to suspend all of that till at least the thirty-first day. All you do for these thirty days is meditate for fifteen minutes in the morning and visualize your movie for five minutes at night.

If you do that, you will have delved enough into your subconscious mind that your inner navigation system will then start taking you in the direction of your dreams. It's worked for me over and over again. Think of these thirty days as an investment—because believe me, they literally will help you find the kind of happiness that money can't buy.

It's important to pick a future time for your movie to take place, but don't make it too far away. I recommend that people don't set the date of their movie any more than three years into the future. When I started doing this kind of visualization, I used five years as a marker, but in reality I got everything I had envisioned in less than three, and I've seen the same thing happen with many other people I've worked with. And I think because of the speed with which things change, the time frames will only get shorter.

"The trouble with our times," quipped French poet Paul Valery, "is that the future is not what it used to be." And if that was true when Valery said it, almost a century ago, it is only more true today. Things are changing so fast that it is difficult to even imagine what kind of world we will be living in just a decade or two from now. It hasn't always been this way. Our great-great-grandparents probably had a pretty good sense of the world their children would be growing up in. As futurist Ray Kurzweil said in a 2003 interview with *What Is Enlightenment?* magazine, "Centuries ago, people didn't even realize that anything was changing at all. They expected their grandchildren to live the same lives that they did, and largely those expectations were borne out. That started to change around the dawn of the Industrial Revolution, two centuries ago." Kurzweil declares that "the most significant change that my investigation as an inventor has uncovered is that *the pace of change is itself accelerating.* People still understand the rate of change to be a constant. In fact it's not a constant . . . change is actually growing exponentially." He estimates that we are doubling the rate of progress every decade, which leads to his mind-boggling calculation that "the twentieth century was like twenty years of change at today's rate of change; in the next twenty years we're going to make five times the progress you saw in the twentieth century; and we'll make twenty thousand years of progress in the twenty-first century, which is almost a thousand times more technical change than we saw in the twentieth century." [2]

Just think about how many of the things you take for granted today didn't even exist twenty years ago—like iPods, HD television, and in-car navigation systems. The first commercial use of e-mail was in 1988. Or take an example like travel: Two hundred years ago, if you wanted to go from America to Europe, it would take months on a ship. In the early days of commercial aviation, you could take a plane that used to take fourteen hours. Then ten hours. Now a regular commercial flight takes six hours.

Moore's Law, named after Intel cofounder George Moore, tells us that the speed of technology is doubling every year, and the cost is halving. Technology is allowing us to see results more quickly than ever before. The way this relates to our discussion of the future is that it means the gap between a desire and the fulfillment of that desire is narrowing at a rapid pace. That's why my advice is that you not make your time frames too long. To look at it from a simply consumerist perspective, if we just assume for a moment that money is not an issue, you really can get almost anything you want—now. One day, when I was staying in my apartment in New York, I started flipping through the phone book out of curiosity to see what I could have delivered to my door within an hour. If I wanted, I could have gotten a new mattress, a gourmet meal, a string quartet, or someone to teach me Italian.

> **‖‖‖**
>
> **When you project your attention into the future, the manifestation of your thoughts into reality is happening at a quicker and quicker pace.**
>
> **‖‖‖**

So when you project your attention into the future, the manifestation of your thoughts into reality is happening at a quicker and quicker pace. If we put our minds on something specific, we get to actually see, in a pretty short time frame, whether we get any results or not. It's not like a few centuries ago where you had to wait years and years to see the fruits of your labor, thoughts, and dreams. Humans are speeding up that process. What I would say now is that it seems that most people I've worked with and coached can turn things around in about six to twelve months. A lot of that has to do with what you believe is possible, and how concrete your vision is to make this process work.

ACT AS IF

There's an old saying: "Act as if." Or, as we often say, "Fake it till you make it." Act as if you were that financial planner just seeing those clients that you love to see; act as if you are the plumber who already has his own business. You have to act as if you are already that person that you want to be.

In my financial firm, I'm notorious for doing this. When we only had $100 million in assets, I'd walk around the office saying we were a $500 million firm. People would say, "We're not a $500 million firm," and I'd say, "Well, in my mind we are, and if I believe it, we'll get there." And I literally took the whole organization with me. Quicker than just about any financial organization I've ever heard about, we became a $500 million company. Then I started walking around saying that we were a $1 billion firm. And people said, "That's a stretch, there are all these obstacles." I'd say, "Forget it. I don't want to hear about any of that. We are a $1 billion firm." And within seven years we went from having zero assets to having a billion dollars in assets, which is pretty much unheard of.

One of my favorite stories about this principle is about the time I decided to do a fund-raiser for autism. I told Dr. Charles Cartwright, the director of the Autism Center at New Jersey Medical School, that I was going to raise $300,000. He said, "How did you come up with that number?" I said, "I don't know, it just sounds like a good start." I didn't know anyone who had that kind of money to spare, and I had no fund-raising experience, but I was convinced we were going to raise the 300 grand. So I got my sister to work for me and we started a committee. We hosted a black-tie dinner, with tickets that included special reserve seating for a concert, and all the money raised above the ticket costs was to go to the charity. The event itself raised $150,000.

Now, I'm rarely wrong when I say that I am going to reach a financial goal. So everyone in my office found it quite amusing that I was only halfway to my goal when the dinner was almost over. We had invited various speakers to come and say a few words during the dinner, and one of the people we had included was the then governor of New Jersey, Richard Cody, because we knew he was going to be in the area of the concert hall that night. We didn't know if he would show up, but about halfway through the evening, we got word from security that he was downstairs having dinner and would like to come up for five minutes and say a few words.

So he came in and addressed everyone. He and his wife do a lot to support mental health initiatives. And he said to me, in front of all the guests gathered there, "I really want to commend you and the center, and I'm going to match, dollar for dollar, everything that you have raised tonight." So we raised our $300,000 on that one event.

GOING BEYOND A DESTINATION

A word of warning about success: I achieved everything I had pictured for myself in my mental movie in less than three years. But this world is a world of duality, and while I firmly believe you can have anything you want from the world, I also have learned that it will come with its opposite to balance it out. If you want a lot of money, it will come with the stress and obligation of having a lot of money. If you want fame, it will come with the stress and obligation of being under a microscope. I got everything I ever wanted and found that I still had no peace and didn't feel successful or any better than before. And the reason was very simple: I wasn't focused on my expression in the world, but on what I could get out of the world.

Your movie has to keep evolving. We are talking about a movie that has to be constantly refilmed. And that's the difficult part. One of my best friends was a computer programmer working in a bank. One day he told me that he wanted to write a book. I suggested he try making a movie—that he spend the next thirty days imagining as vividly and as concretely as possible "a day in the life of Andy as a published author." I told him to take it as far as he could—even to imagine the cover design. He kept coming up with all the reasons it would never work. So I told him it was critical that for the next thirty days that he not focus on the obstacles while going through this process.

It's not that the obstacles might not be real and significant; it's just that this thirty-day period is *only* about setting your destination. It's kind of like picking a vacation spot—at first, you just look for the place you will have the most fun. Later, of course, you will deal with all the practicalities, but they're not necessarily part of the initial process. Allow your creative imagination to flow freely in picking a destination for your future self in the same way you would pick a destination for your summer break.

||||

The reason I felt no peace was simple: I wasn't focused on my expression in the world but on what I could get out of the world.

||||

Within six months of our conversation, my friend Andy had published his book, and sold his first copy. Six months later he was in a total funk again. When I met up with him for dinner, I found out he never evolved his movie past the moment the book was published. This is the problem with making your movie about a destination. For Andy it was about a book, not about how he would use that book to express himself in the world. This is the downside of the law of attraction—you can use your mind to get anything you want, but it's not necessarily going to enrich your life.

Andy had all these expectations about what he would feel like if he wrote this book. At the root was his desire to help people feel better, but for him it came with a price. He wanted to feel better about himself. He didn't realize that this is an ongoing process and not a destination. He should have visualized using the book in lectures and seminars, so that as his own movie evolved he would be helping people through these engagements. Life is a journey, and this process never works when it's only about you reaching a fixed destination.

It is the same principle as when you go to a personal trainer at the gym. A good trainer won't just have you doing the same exercises over and over again forever. The trainer will encourage you to stick with a certain plan until you get results, and then change your routine, otherwise you are likely to find yourself bored, and your results will plateau.

I see this all the time, even with people who have had a lot of success with using this visualization technique. They get what they wanted within six months or a year, and then hit a downward spiral once they get what they wanted because they have no idea what to do next. You can't use the technique simply because you think the final scene will give you eternal happiness; it doesn't work that way. Your movie, your mental vision of the future you, has to be constantly evolving, and in the end we find that it is actually the fact of being in that state of creative tension and striving that brings us true fulfillment and joy.

IIII

The downside of the law of attraction is that you can use your mind to get anything you want, but it's not necessarily going to enrich your life.

IIII

Every couple of years, I ask myself who I want to become. This is something we naturally do as children. Do you remember how one week you wanted to be a fireman or a nurse and the next you were determined to be a mountain climber or a ballerina? We lose this sense of self-creating vision as we grow up, instead growing accustomed to and even feeling victimized by who we already are, feeling powerless to significantly change. So I always give myself the freedom to reinvent who I want to be.

When I was studying economics in college, I learned about the idea of an "S-curve" that shows how businesses or new ideas emerge and develop in the marketplace. It's called an S-curve because it looks kind of like a letter *s* that has been stretched horizontally. The basic idea is that there is a long initial process of getting an idea into the marketplace, during which the line is basically flat. Once the idea is accepted by the marketplace there is usually a five- to seven-year period of vertical growth, and the line moves steeply or gradually upward, before it levels off and then starts to decline.

IIII

It is the fact of being in that state of creative tension and striving that brings us true fulfillment and joy.

IIII

This idea always seemed to me to apply not just to economics, but to myself. That image of the S-curve kept me thinking about the fact that if I didn't continually evolve my expression in the world, eventually I would be guaranteed to hit a period of decline. In business, we are taught always to introduce a new S-curve during the later stage of the vertical development of your business plan's prior S-curve. In the same way, once your movie has become your reality, and you are enjoying the fruits of your success, that is the moment to make a new movie.

Believe me, although it logically makes sense, you may not feel like doing it at the moment when it's most important that you do. It's easy to envision a movie about what you want to become when you are miserable. But when you've worked hard to get somewhere and are happy at least momentarily, you will probably feel like you just want to relax and forget about the future. But that's like making a half-million a year and not wanting to bother saving for retirement. It doesn't make any sense, and it will guarantee you that your happiness will only be a temporary state, not a lasting return on your investment.

So get used to moving out of your comfort zone over and over again. It's hard to make a new movie, especially if you are someone who thrives on security. It means making a conscious decision about what's most important to you—what you want your life to look like in the future or how comfortable you are with your life now. While comfort brings security, it never brings deep satisfaction. As the saying goes, "If we're not growing, we're dying."

THE
FOURTH
PILLAR

EXPANDING YOUR AWARENESS

You only have what you give. It is by
spending yourself that you become rich.
—*ISABELLE ALLENDE*

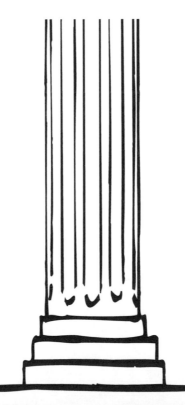

CHAPTER TEN

GIVING

*The only ones among you who will be
really happy are those who will have sought
and found how to serve.*

—*ALBERT SCHWEITZER*

MANY OF MY CLIENTS TELL ME THAT THEY DON'T JUST want to get out of debt, budget their expenses, invest wisely, or save for retirement. They also want to be able to give: to become a philanthropist, start a foundation, or just make regular donations to a charity of their choice. People with religious beliefs see this objective as an important part of their financial plan. Most religious groups encourage charitable giving or *tithing,* and some are even specific that it should account for at least 10 percent of your income.

In our attention investment plan, I recommend the same thing—in fact, I see it as essential to success. If attention is the new currency, you need to be giving at least 10 percent of your attention freely to others. Again, it may sound simple, but when you try it, you will be surprised at just how much attention you tend to keep to yourself, and how little you give away without expectation of return.

For most of us, our awareness and attention are caught up in our own minds. We are aware of our own needs and wants and we can't get out of that loop. The first three pillars are about regaining control of your attention, spending it wisely, and investing it in your future. So to continue our metaphor of a financial plan for your attention, this fourth pillar would be philanthropy. In the conventional sense, philanthropy means "love for mankind, usually demonstrated by giving money to, or doing work for, other people." In this context, we replace the currency of money with that of attention. So the fourth pillar is about expanding our awareness by giving our attention to others.

When it comes to financial philanthropy, most people who give generously are those who already consider themselves wealthy. This makes sense—if you can't support your own family and pay the daily bills, you won't be writing $10,000 checks to even the most worthy of causes. But this is where things work differently when it comes to attention. I encourage you to give from the very beginning of your transformational journey, even though it may seem counterintuitive at times.

A few years ago, I went on a trip to a Land Rover training school in North Carolina. It was quite an experience. You get to drive a car that is smarter than you are when it comes to driving on rough terrain. The instructor told me, "If you're going downhill and you start losing grip, don't brake." I thought he was kidding, but he wasn't. He explained that with this car, you actually had to step on the gas, which is so contrary to everything we are usually taught. If you're flying down a hill and you start losing control, your natural tendency is to step on the brake. But in this car, the trick was to step on the gas. The tires would then grab onto the dirt, engage, and provide the stability and grounding you needed. In the same way, the fourth pillar is counterintuitive, but it works. Just when your instincts tell you to try to hold on to as much as you can get, you have to do completely the opposite, and find a way to *give*.

This is a simple principle, but it is one that often goes against many of our deeply imprinted habits. Indeed, the fourth pillar says that the key to true success is finding a way to give. And I don't just mean that once you are successful you can donate to a worthy cause. I mean that giving has to become an integral part of your unique creative expression. Giving is not just a nice afterthought to success—it is, in my experience, the very key to true success, fulfillment, and lasting happiness. Simply being concerned about our own selfish needs and desires is a certain recipe for unhappiness, while being of service and giving to others is where true fulfillment is found. This is the whole point of the fourth pillar, the first three pillars prepare us for the fourth.

> **||||**
>
> **Giving is not just a nice afterthought to success; it is the very key to success.**
>
> **||||**

Most people are deeply convinced that they need to keep control of their energy and use it to get what they want. They go through each day consciously or unconsciously saying to themselves, "I need to think about getting what I want, otherwise I'll never get it." What we've done in the first three pillars is to lay out a track for the subconscious mind to follow, through focusing on what you want. But once your subconscious has been trained in this way, you need to let go of that. Once you are playing your movie in your head every night before you go to bed, once you've entered your destination into your navigation system, you need to let go of it. And you can then put all your attention on others.

This is a scary thing for some people, because many of us think we need to use our minds to get what we want as much as possible. When people I coach say something like this, I like to ask: How's that working out for you so far? As the problems we face individually and collectively continue to worsen, it is becoming increasingly clear that it's not working out, yet unfortunately many people still believe it's the only way.

What I'm asking you to do is to flip that old idea on its head. Put the address of your destination—that place you want to get to in the near future—into your navigation system and then put all your attention on driving right now. And what happens when you are driving your car is the navigation system says, "Okay, now turn right." It's making your path clear so that you can put all your attention on driving. Here's the key: Let your subconscious mind work for you. It can get you to your destination while you use your conscious mind to shine the light of attention on every individual that you can interact with during the day, spending as much of your attention currency on others as you can sustain. You'll find that when you are completely present, you recognize opportunities in the moment that further express yourself in the world. In the past you would have missed these moments because your attention was too busy internally wandering.

> ▊▊▊▊
>
> **When you are completely present, you recognize opportunities in the moment that further express yourself in the world.**
>
> ▊▊▊▊

When you learn to practice the fourth pillar in this way, you will find that your subconscious mind and your conscious mind will be able to work together exponentially faster than any mental effort that you are accustomed to. And not only will you be more present—you'll be much happier in the present moment, too. As one Zen saying goes, "When you have one foot in the past and one in the future, you are pissing on the present!"

If you remember, I related the third pillar to investment. And as any financial planner will tell you, once you have invested your money wisely and you know it is being well managed, you need to leave it alone. I have clients who drive themselves crazy watching the daily gyrations of the market as it takes their portfolio up and down in the short term. Their attention is consumed by worrying about whether they made the wrong decisions in the past and what they can do to make different decisions in the future. In fact, if you have a good financial planner and a well-diversified portfolio, the daily ups and downs shouldn't affect your long-term success. The markets generally tend upward, and one of the reasons you have a financial planner is so that your attention can be freed from that kind of day-to-day worry.

In the same way, once you have invested your attention in your own future by making your movie—that is, by visualizing the person you want to be—and playing that movie to yourself each night, then you can take your attention away from that for the rest of your day and start to focus it on giving.

WHAT TO GIVE

When I speak about giving, I am not necessarily talking about money or even time and effort. Most people take this advice the wrong way at first. They think that I'm saying that you have to volunteer at a soup kitchen or write a check to the Humane Society, and while those are good things to do, that's not what I'm talking about. The currency of this model, remember, is attention. And the truth is that what everyone is craving in the world is someone else's attention. It might be a parent's attention, it might be the public's attention, the boss's attention, a loved one's attention, but people literally are craving attention. So this pillar uses that same currency. It is about Expanding Your Awareness, giving your attention, and therefore your energy, to others. And the secret of the fourth pillar, while counterintuitive, is that doing so is the greatest possible source of energy you could ever find.

I want you to think for a moment about those times in your life when you've truly *given* something—to others, to your community, to the planet. Aren't moments like that among the happiest memories you hold? Think about how you feel after a day when you've unreservedly given to others—whether it's your kids, a friend, or a complete stranger in need of help. In times like that, you may feel tired, physically, but there is often a surprising sense of energy, freedom, and joy that is released in the process. Then contrast that to how you feel after a day spent trying to get stuff for yourself— a shopping trip, a long day trying to make sales, a tough negotiation for a pay rise. You probably feel drained, exhausted, as if you've spent every last drop of your energy in the chase.

I have a client who is a psychiatrist who works with kids with learning disabilities and emotional issues. She frequently works twelve-hour days with these kids and then often stops to visit one of her nineteen grandchildren, many of whom live in the same town as her. She tells me that she feels more drained trying to make vacation plans for a week away with her husband than she does working these long days giving her attention away.

It's important to remember that the Four Pillars are all connected into one integrated life. So when we think about giving, don't think of it as an extra or an afterthought. For success to be sustainable, giving needs to become an integral part of a person's unique creative expression. If your unique expression is only aimed at satisfying your own desires and wants and your fundamental motive is to get something back for yourself, you will not find lasting happiness and fulfillment. You will burn out. You might seem to get what you want initially, but over the long haul you will not be able to sustain it.

Let's revisit the metaphor of going to the gym. If you tell yourself, I'm going to go to the gym and pump some iron so that I can look good, that's a very shortsighted approach. You're really not helping your body because you are only interested in using it to get attention. I'm sure you know people like this. They start a workout program and then, as soon as they start looking a little good, they get burned out and stop going until they gain the weight back again, and then they reluctantly show up to start over. It becomes an on-again, off-again cycle. But you probably also know people who go to the gym regularly, and who are there because they care about their health and long-term well-being. If you go to the gym because you are focused on the overall health of the body, then the body will perform for you for a very long time.

The same thing is true out in the world. If all we are focused on is what we can get from the world, we will find that our cravings are never satisfied. As soon as we get what we want, we want something else. And as soon as we get that, we want something else. Eventually, if you are lucky, like I was, and get what you thought would make you happy, you will likely come to realize that ultimately there isn't anything "out there" that will give you the fulfillment you long for—and the endless loop begins to burn itself out.

The other way people come to this realization is a harder path. They reach a place of utter desperation where they have nothing, and then they discover a source of fulfillment within. One of the most popular spiritual teachers of our time, Eckhart Tolle, described such a moment in his own life: "Everything felt so alien, so hostile, and so utterly meaningless that it created in me a deep loathing of the world. . . . I could feel that a deep longing for annihilation, for nonexistence, was now becoming much stronger

▌▌▌▌

You begin to realize that there isn't anything "out there" that will give you the fulfillment you long for, and the endless loop begins to burn itself out.

▌▌▌▌

than the instinctive desire to continue to live."[1] This moment of despair, of recognizing that "I cannot live with myself any longer," was the catalyst for a profound transformation into a state of such bliss, peace, and joy. As he observed, "Nothing I ever *did* could possibly add anything to what I already had."[2]

Either of these scenarios have the power to shock you out of the cycle. Maybe you haven't reached either of these extreme situations, but you nonetheless realize that you are caught in the cycle. The good news is that you don't need to wait. You can step out of it right now. And the way to do so is by being completely focused not on what you are getting but on what you are contributing. Paradoxically, the more energy you put out, the more energy you find that you have. It's like a boomerang— you throw it out and mysteriously, it comes back to you. When you are focused on how much energy you're getting from the world, whether it is money or sex or power, whatever it might be, you literally burn out because you are not putting anything into the vast system of life that sustains you and everything else. On the other hand, if you focus on giving to the world and those around you, you are pumping energy into the system, and because you are part of that system, you will find that you also benefit.

If you focus on giving to the world and those around you, you are pumping energy into the system.

People always ask me why I do so many seminars for free. They wonder why I don't charge for my time. But I know that in the currency that really matters to me, I will be more than compensated. I know that the energy I put into them will come back. Everything comes back when it is freely given. As Ralph Waldo Emerson wrote, "It is one of the beautiful compensations of this life that no man can sincerely try to help another without helping himself."

CHAPTER ELEVEN

BEYOND SUCCESS

All men seek one goal: success or happiness.
The only way to achieve true success is to ex-
press yourself completely in service to society.

—*ARISTOTLE*

MY UNDERSTANDING OF THE POWER OF EXPANDING
your awareness came about when I started realizing
that my unique expression in the world was helping
other people find peace and happiness. How it started was that I
would sit with clients during what we call a "fact-finding session."
The idea was that I was there simply to get information, to gather
data like their Social Security number, date of birth, place of work,
the kind of house they lived in, their income, assets, and so on.

One day, I was getting out of my car and about to walk into a
prospect's house to try and sell some term life insurance. I was way
behind on my bills, and my mind was going on and on about how
much I needed the sale. Desperation poured out of me as I caught
my reflection in the car window. I stopped and looked hard at that
reflection and said to myself, "Who would want to buy anything
from you? Look at how desperate you look!"

I thought of the successful people in my office and realized that
to some extent, they all had a confidence about themselves that I
sorely lacked. And so I decided in that moment that I needed to

drop my desperate, needy attitude and walk into this prospect's house with the confidence of someone who didn't want anything. I began to think of myself as an actor playing the cool, confident star. Images of Eastwood and Pacino flashed through my mind.

I took one last look at my reflection and saw that I had taken on an air of serenity. That's when I began to realize that I really didn't need anything, that deep down there was nothing for me to get. I dropped my self-doubt, worry, and need to make a sale. I became still and quiet. And then as I approached more clients this way and began putting all my attention on the other person, without any desire or expectation for myself personally, my meetings started to transform.

I had to leave behind my own agenda, my desire to make a sale. But the results were something far more fulfilling. To put it simply, people began to open up in ways they never opened up before. The fact-finding sessions started to become therapy sessions, and I started to carry the same principle through to all my client meetings. Clients began to express things that maybe they had bottled up for years: challenges that they had at home, worries or fears that were eating away at them. And many people started to tell me that they felt an intense calm within ten or fifteen minutes of being in a meeting with me. Sometimes just the fact that I was able to help people achieve that calm became the purpose for me being there. It wasn't that we talked about the stock market or how much life insurance they needed or what their investments would be. All my meetings started to become these cleansing and bonding sessions. And the better I got at it, the more deeply I was able to give of my attention, the more there seemed to be a reward for the both of us.

For me, it was an unbelievably transformative experience to just be able to give someone else all of my attention. Even if nothing is said, something happens when you do that with another human being that is radically different from the ways we usually interact.

As I was going through my crisis of disillusionment with my own worldly success, I discovered at the same time that the more I gave to others, the more complete and happy I felt—and, oddly enough, the more I got in return. I had more than I ever needed materially and it hadn't made me happy, so I changed my modus operandi. I focused on meditating, finding more silence and peace, and sharing that with other people. And still my income kept growing. I was accomplishing more and more, and getting more accolades in the world. Not only that, but the more I was in that space, the more energy I focused on other people and the less I put on myself, the more I was able to do. I became chairman of the autism center and started a fund-raiser that we now hold every year, raising over a million dollars for autism research. And as more doors opened up for me, the more my business grew.

My frame of mind going into a meeting with another human being is, how am I needed here? And the only way I could figure out how I'm needed is to get completely quiet in my own mind, just listen, and put all my attention on the other person. And usually, the way that I'm needed reveals itself. Maybe I'm needed just to listen for that hour. Maybe I'm needed to give some advice or point somebody in the right direction. But the only way I seem to come to that point when I know how I'm needed and what I have to give is by first getting completely quiet and having no interest in what I get out of it.

I literally started to go to client meetings with absolutely no regard for needing to make money or anything else. I would simply walk in and shut out the outside world for the hour or two that I was with my client and put 100 percent of my attention on the other person. This is the key thing to understand about Expanding Your Awareness. It's not just about a one-way act of charity. It's a mutually beneficial care for the one system we're all part of. That's why I love the famous quote that is attributed to an aboriginal woman, Lila Watson: "If you are coming to help me, you are wasting your time. But if you are coming because your liberation is bound up with mine, then let us work together." We need to begin to understand that our liberation, our success, our fulfillment, our happiness is bound up with one another, and with the planetary system we share. We're all part of one system, and if we're all part of one system, in order for anyone to get anything out of the system, the system has to be healthy. It's just like a thermodynamic system. If there is something sucking energy from the system all the time and there is no source of new energy coming into the system, then eventually the system dies due to lack of energy. The same is true of our ability to operate in the world. If I'm only concerned about consuming personally from the world, then I burn out that small system that I am a part of and eventually it dies. And this principle operates even when only two people are together: We are both part of one system, here to have a working relationship together. So if we are going to have a working relationship together, whether it's about your financial planning or my way of earning a living, we are still part of one system.

IIII

If we're all part of one system, in order for anyone to get anything out of the system, the system has to be healthy.

IIII

Often, I go into business meetings and when the other person comes in, I can see that the person is completely focused on what he's going to get out of it and what he wants. People expect to meet someone on the other side of the table who is coming with the same mentality, who is going to fight for "what's in it for them." This kind of "taking" energy is used to being met with resistance and then fighting that resistance to get what it wants. But then I come in with an unconditional mentality of giving, and it completely defuses the aggression. Clients transform in front of my eyes, and we both come out of the meeting as winners.

When I gave the seminar in which these Four Pillars first emerged, I was in that space of not wanting anything out of it. Everyone who took my card after that seminar, I coached for free. And I have no doubt that the reason that presentation had such an impact, on me and so many others, is because I realized I was just there in service. For some reason, most people think it's very difficult to just be in service. The truth is, it's a very easy process. If you can just let go of wanting anything for yourself, which is the hard part, the service itself comes naturally.

A BEYOND SUCCESS STORY

Not long ago, I got together for lunch with a fellow who had once come to me for a few coaching sessions. It had been a few years since I had seen him, and when he walked in, I was immediately struck by how different he looked. He looked happy, confident, relaxed. I remembered him seeming depressed and nervous about his future. As he put it, "I was in that space of searching, wanting something. And I felt that you could give me something. You're a successful guy, you have this peace, and you were very generous with me, and I just wanted to get something from you. It was this desperate need. I thought, 'Jeff's going to give me something to complete me.'"

I asked him, "What changed?" He said, "It all started with the seed you planted." He told me that as a result of our coaching sessions, he had found the sense of purpose he had been searching for all of his life. He reminded me that I had asked him, "What is your life about? What do you really want to do, ultimately?" In that moment, he had realized that all of the things he thought he needed—more business, a new house, a new car—didn't really mean anything to him. He had said to me: "I want to be a force of good in the world. I want to be somebody who is helping people in some way. I want to be a part of the solution."

And I had told him, "Forget about all your goals; just put them out of your mind and forget all of them. I want you to get up in the morning and be that person you want to be, no matter who shows up in your life, no matter what happens."

He took my advice to heart and, as he described to me over lunch, it completely transformed his life. "I stopped this urge to get more and to do more and be so unsatisfied with myself," he said. "That doesn't mean that I don't have goals—in fact, my business has almost doubled, and I'm doing some of the best work I've done in my entire life because I'm putting so much into it and coming at it with a totally different perspective. I'm not trying to get business anymore. I'm showing up and being this person I wanted to be, and business is flooding in to me. And it's important to me to do a good job for my clients. If I'm going to serve, I really want to serve them well. And there are lots of things I want, but I don't feel like I need them now to complete myself or to enhance myself in any way."

I commented on how different he looked, how his newfound sense of purpose was obvious even in his appearance. He smiled. "I can't believe that just three years ago I was looking for work. I couldn't even get a job. I thought I was over the hill, my life was over, I had missed the boat." I love the image he used to describe his transformation: "I almost went into a time machine that day. You projected me off into the future of the person I wanted to be. You took me to the future—but what I realized was that the future was actually the next day. I was transformed right away. Granted, there was a lot of work to do, and I had challenges, but now I knew that the purpose of my life was to be that person, and I didn't have to wait to make a lot of money or get anywhere before I could do that."

This man is just one of many such transformations I've seen in people who discover this shift in perspective. In one sense, it's very simple, but it can be such a difficult thing to communicate to people. Often, we are coming into the world as takers, but we don't even know it. We're just indoctrinated into that way of being. Many of us, like my friend, have a deep sense of the person we would like to be, but that image is always followed by an *"if. . . ."* We think, "I could be that person if I had enough money, if I just had more time, if my business would be successful and I was less stressed."

> **||||**
>
> **We spend our lives waiting to get something from the world so we can show up as the person we always knew we could be.**
>
> **||||**

Unfortunately, too many of us spend our whole lives waiting to get something from the world so that we can show up as the person we always knew we could be. Deep in our hearts we think there's something missing. But when we flip that mindset, we discover that by becoming a giver rather than a taker, we can change the world, literally, one person at a time.

BREAKING THE SCARCITY MINDSET

The idea that giving actually increases energy and taking actually decreases it is very difficult for many people to grasp. The problem has to do with our mindset. Most of us are caught up in a cultural mindset that says "there's not enough for everybody." In actuality, most of us reading this book probably don't live in a context where we don't have the resources to live and feed our families.

Numerous studies attest that the average standard of living has risen dramatically in the United States over the past fifty years, measuring income, percentage of the population considered middle-class or higher, value of money, diversity of product choice, living space, working environments, leisure time, and even crime rates. Yet the percentage of people who consider themselves satisfied with their lives has changed very little, if at all. In his book *The Mind of the Market,* evolutionary economist Michael Shermer cites a 1994 Princeton Research Associates study that found that less than 50 percent of Americans feel they have enough money to lead satisfactory lives.[1] "We live with scarcity as an underlying assumption," writes Lynne Twist in *The Soul of Money,* pointing out that this often unconscious mindset of "not enough" and "more is better" plagues the rich as much as the poor.[2]

It's in our language: *Money doesn't grow on trees; you gotta get your slice of the pie.* All the ways we speak about resources and money are based in this conviction of scarcity. And if we believe in scarcity, then we believe we have to fight other people for those scarce resources. As long as we believe in scarcity, and as long as we hold the deep and unconscious assumption that "I've got to get and hold on to as much as possible," we will not be focused on giving back and contributing to the health of the system. Maybe in the small area where we live the system may seem to be doing just fine, but look at the world. The world is burning out. There don't seem to be enough resources, like food, for everybody. And it's not actually true. It just appears that way because the small minority of us who are the most fortunate and privileged are somehow unable to be satisfied with what we have. Instead of focusing on giving our energy back to the world and to the vast majority who don't have what they need, we keep taking and taking and taking.

It's very difficult to break free of this scarcity mentality that most of us have been born with—the conviction that "there's not enough and I've got to work my butt off, I've got to run on the gerbil wheel as much as I can to make sure I get enough so I can keep up with everybody else." And it's not just about money or resources. In the West, where we don't have to worry about these basic survival needs, the scarcity mentality is how we relate to the deeper currency that I've been speaking about throughout this book: attention.

IIII

In the West, where we worry less about basic survival needs, the scarcity mentality is how we relate to the deeper currency of attention.

IIII

As we've discussed, human beings spend most of their days with their attention being pulled in millions of directions. It's very rare that people have attention given to them without anything wanted in return. Most people who give you their attention want something back for it. They're doing it as an exchange. Remember, where attention goes, energy flows. Most of the time when people get together, they are trying to take energy from one another. That's the dynamic, the energy flow that exists in most of the world.

So we're stuck in this paradigm where we think that the void and emptiness that we feel inside can be filled by something outside of us. Whether it's money, food, sex, drugs, or attention from other people, we are seeking something to fill the void so that we will feel we have "enough." But the truth is, we'll never get to that point.

As a financial planner who deals with many people, from those with moderate incomes to those who make over a million dollars a year, I can tell you that there is no "enough" in this mindset. There is nothing to get out there—no amount of money or other people's attention—that will satisfy that ache, that void, that emptiness that we all feel inside. The truth is we all feel that ache and that emptiness because we are supposed to be *givers* of energy; we're supposed to be of service; we're supposed to be using our energy in service to others. Because we've flipped the switch and are consumed with taking as much as we can from the world and everyone else around us, we've created this black hole inside us. No matter how much we are sucked into our inner black hole, it will infinitely keep wanting more.

Encouraging readers to change their scarcity-based relationship with money, Lynne Twist writes that "sufficiency resides inside of each of us. . . . In our relationship with money, it is using money in a way that expresses our integrity; using it in a way that *expresses* value rather than determines value."[3] I would say that the same principle applies to the currency of attention: The only way that we ever come to a place where we feel fulfilled and discover the sense of happiness that we're all looking for is when we flip the switch—and start *giving* our energy away, using our attention as a means of expression outward, rather than trying to get attention from others in order to feel valued. The more we can give it away, the more fulfilled and happy we will be.

▮▮▮▮

The only way to fulfillment is to start *giving* our energy away, using our attention as a means of expression outward rather than trying to get attention from others in order to feel valued.

▮▮▮▮

The most exciting thing about this flip is that we discover that while taking always reaches a saturation point, giving is infinite. Think about when you desperately want some ice cream. There can be a tremendous thrill in the anticipation of that bowl of creamy, sugary delight, and initially the experience of eating the ice cream can fulfill the longing you feel in a blissfully satisfying way. But once you've eaten one bowl, if you keep eating more, you'll quickly find that what was pleasurable only a minute before becomes unpleasant and leaves you feeling slightly sick. That's saturation.

With giving, this never happens. I've never been in a situation where I'm so sick of giving that I just don't want to do it anymore. The feeling you get when you see the look on the face of someone you've really helped—there is no end to how happy that can make you.

I'm not saying it will be easy. So much of the world is operating on the belief that we have to take as much as we can. But it doesn't take a rocket scientist to look around the world, especially at America, and see how many seemingly successful people are miserable. Even people who make it to the top— rock stars, CEOs, actresses, lottery winners—who seemingly have what everyone else wants, are often miserable, depressed, and sometimes even suicidal. The system is not working, and there's only one other way it can work. We can either be takers or givers.

When we look at the problem on this scale, it can seem overwhelming. But the only way this vast, deeply embedded system of taking is going to shift is by individuals turning themselves around. It's the same principle that works in my client meetings: When we meet the taking attitude with no resistance, something is released. It starts on an energetic level; it then translates into visible change in the material world. You can see this starting to happen in business, as the corporate machines slowly begin to wake up to the value of giving back.

This has been especially true in more recent years when it comes to the environment. What the *New York Times* called "the emerging convergence of for-profit money-making and nonprofit mission" is more evident every day, with new books, articles, and advertising campaigns promoting both the virtue and value of sustainable or "green" business. "I think what people are increasingly looking for, whether in the for-profit or nonprofit sector, is how you harness the vitality and promise of capitalism in a way that's more fair to everyone," said Juliana Eades, president of the New Hampshire Community Loan Fund, who was quoted in the *New York Times* article.[4] From GE's multibillion-dollar "Ecomagination" initiative, to Wal-Mart's promotion of "earth friendly" products, to Unilever's work to help feed children in Asia, the behemoths of the corporate world are realizing that they can't ignore the social and environmental impact of their business.

You may be cynical about the motives of big business for "going green," but the point is, they are doing it, with more high-profile companies getting on the train every day. This is not a naive way to look at it—as Stonyfield Farms CEO Gary Hirshberg, author of *Stirring It Up: How to Make Money and Save the World,* pointed out, "When these companies go into organics, it's not because they are doing it for moral reasons. They are doing it for financial reasons and, therefore, they have a financial stake in its success."[5]

And if companies are going green for financial reasons, that means this change is *consumer* driven—which means it is *attention* driven, when translated into the terms of the new currency. Investment bank Goldman Sachs now analyses the environmental, social, and management performance of companies in the same way that it analyzes financial performance. Why? Because investors wanted to know.

The growing desire among "conscience-driven consumers" to integrate their spiritual and social values with business and financial success is reflected in trends such as the exponential growth of "socially responsible investment," or SRI (over 5,000 percent in less than two decades), the surge of nonprofits devoted to "spirit in the workplace" (from just a few hundred at the beginning of the new millennium to over 1,200 in 2005), and the growing number of leading business schools, including Harvard, Columbia, and Stanford, that are incorporating modules on spirituality into their courses and MBA programs. According to Patricia Aburdene, author of the best-selling *Megatrends 2010,* this development has a simple reason behind it: "The personal quest for Spirit has hit critical mass." And she sees this as the force that is poised to transform corporate culture: "Spirituality in business, having quietly blossomed for decades, is an established trend that is about to morph into a megatrend."[6]

There is much more that could be said about the transformation of business, but that is beyond the scope of this book. My point, however, is that all of this starts with you—and how you spend your attention and energy. It starts with how you and I treat each other as human beings, and with the understanding that in a relationship with each other, we don't always have to be taking. We have to start there. If we don't start at this most basic of levels, the change will only be superficial. We can give money, we can give time, we can give effort, and those will make a short-term difference, but they won't erode the foundations of the system itself. And they won't bring you the happiness you so deeply crave. So the first step is learning how to be still for a moment and give another person your full attention.

GIVING ATTENTION

The great spiritual author J. Krishnamurti was a master of attention. In his book *This Light in Oneself: True Meditation,* he challenges the reader:

> Have you ever given attention to something totally? Are you giving attention to what the speaker is saying? Or are you listening with a comparative mind that has already acquired knowledge and is comparing what is being said to what you already know? Are you interpreting what is being said according to your own

knowledge, your own tendency, your own prejudice? That is not attention, is it? If you give complete attention, with your body, with your nerves, with your mind, with your whole being, there is no center from which you are standing, there is only attention. That attention is complete silence . . . give your attention to what is being said, so that the very act of listening is a miracle of attention.[7]

I always remember that the few people who made me feel good and safe and secure as a kid were the ones who actually gave me their full attention when they would engage with me. That's a rare thing; most adults don't give their full attention to a child. I remember very distinctly one old man at the temple where I went to Hebrew school. He must have been eighty years old, and he didn't speak at all. But when I would come to the temple, he would just sit with me, or walk around the temple with me. He had the most gentle, soulful eyes I'd ever seen, and when I looked at him, he completely gave me his full attention in a deeper way than I've ever experienced, really, for the rest of my life. It left a profound impression on me at such a young age, because it was so different from anything else that I experienced on a daily basis.

Later in life, as I began to discover the power of attention, I often thought about that old man and asked myself, if he could have such a profound impact on me as a child, what would it mean for those around me and the world at large if I could operate from that same way of being? I find over and over again that it's the most profound thing that happens to me in my life—when I can get completely in that space of almost reverence and surrender to giving my full attention to another human being. It happens most often through coaching. Because I've coached free of charge for the last couple of years, I know that I'm going in there with little or no expectation of anything, and there's little expectation on the client's part as well, so it allows this space to occur.

THE ART OF LISTENING

The DVD version of the 1994 film *Pulp Fiction* includes a few deleted scenes that Quentin Tarantino chose not to use in the final cut. One of these scenes, in particular, came to mind as I sat down to write this chapter. It is entitled "The Interview." In this scene, Mia Wallace (played by Uma Thurman) assumes the role of Barbara Walters as she "interviews" Vincent Vega (played by John Travolta). With video camera in hand, Mia asks Vincent a simple yet profound question: "In conversation, do you listen or wait to talk?" To this, Vincent thoughtfully responds, "I have to admit that I wait to talk—but I'm trying hard to listen."

The only way you can put your attention on the other person is by learning to listen in silence. And *silence doesn't only mean refraining from speaking.* It also means quieting the ongoing dialogue in your own head—the mental noise—so that you can focus on the other person and what he or she is communicating to you. This is where your practice of meditation can serve you well in real-life situations.

It's hard to believe there are so many ways to approach something as seemingly simple as listening, but I estimate there are actually three kinds of listeners.

1. **THE "WAITING TO TALK" LISTENER.** This person is merely waiting for his chance to speak. He hears just enough to tell his own story about the subject being discussed. Conversations with these people often morph into "Who can top this?" storytelling sessions.

2. **THE "ACTIVE" LISTENER.** This person may have read an article about listening, or taken a sales class. She is constantly shaking or nodding her head or saying: "Uh-huh. . . . Yes.

Yes." Perhaps she took an "advanced sales class" and is "mirroring" the other person's body language (while at the same time calculating her anticipated commission or thinking about the errand she needs to run later). All the while, she hasn't heard a word the other party has said.

3. **THE SILENT LISTENER AND COUNSELOR.** This person has learned to silence his internal dialogue and make eye contact. The only words he speaks are open-ended questions designed to dig deeper and elicit more information from the other person.

Have you ever noticed that the words *listen* and *silent* are spelled with the same letters? I think this is appropriate, because they mean the same thing. Have you ever talked to someone and walked away feeling enriched because they were such a good listener, even if they were a complete stranger? This talent is what accounts for some of the best psychologists in the world and some of the best salespeople. Interestingly, it is also the trait most people refer to in a great leader: the ability to listen. Great leaders listen and give us the attention we need.

❚❚❚❚

Great leaders listen and give us the attention we need.

❚❚❚❚

In the seventeenth century, the French philosopher René Descartes said, "I think, therefore I am." But if you want to be a successful listener, the other person must become the center of your universe. Therefore, from this day forward, your mindset must be one that allows you to be open and receptive. You must quiet your thinking and allow yourself to silently listen. To paraphrase Descartes: "I think, therefore I am . . . a poor listener."

My clients call me a buoy of calm in an ocean of turbulence.

Once I arrived for an appointment with a doctor client when he had just gotten home from work. He'd had a bad day, got home late, and was running around trying to get ready for me. The doctor and his wife were frazzled, and their eight-year-old daughter was bouncing off the walls, happy to have her parents home and craving their attention. I remember being acutely aware of how much these people just needed calm; they needed stillness. It was one of the first moments where I really started to put my attention consciously on my clients. I gave my attention 100 percent to this family. I don't remember what we spoke about; I think I mostly just listened to them. But within ten minutes, the doctor's daughter fell asleep on her mother's lap, and the mother leaned back in her chair. The doctor loosened his tie, his breathing calmed, and the frenzied atmosphere in the room relaxed. He turned to me at the end of the appointment and said I must have hypnotized his family. Half joking, he asked me if I could come and do the same thing at 5 p.m. every day! This is the power of our attention. Each of us can command it, and because it is the world's greatest commodity, we can actually change the course of the world by learning to control our attention and using it as a gift for others.

||||

Have some faith that the universe has brought you and the other person together for a more important reason than what you can get out of it in the moment.

||||

Have some faith that the universe has brought you and the other person together for a more important reason than what you can get out of it in the moment. And if that's true, the only way you are going to see that purpose and reason is to get quiet and silent and put your attention on the other person. And then see what happens. If you just try it, I assure you things will become completely different.

The first thing that people often say is, "But I'm going to get walked all over!" And I always say, "Absolutely not." What happens is that when the other person doesn't meet with resistance, he backs down from his fixed position, creating a space for something new to occur, for both people to actually work together for a common purpose, for both people to win, for the whole system to benefit.

People assume that if they come from a position that is not fixed, they are going to get taken advantage of. But actually the opposite is true. It often becomes easier to say "No" to something that you see isn't going to work out because there's not a sense of desperation driving you to try and get more business. It's easier to protect yourself and make the right decisions when you are not coming from that needy place. So, for example, you might be going to a meeting, listening to the other person's proposal with your full attention, and then saying, "No, I can't do that; it wouldn't be beneficial for both of us." It's not about you walking in and giving away the farm.

When you're giving your attention, you'll know exactly what decision to make when it comes to business or relationships.

When I say giving, I'm only talking about giving your attention to the other person; I'm not talking about anything in form or matter on top of that. Give your attention completely to the other person—and then see what happens. When you're in that space, you'll know exactly what decision to make when it comes to business or relationships. The other person might need to hear "No, I'm not interested in this deal."

Initially, it may be easier to practice the art of listening with strangers. There is such an established energy pattern in long-standing relationships, whether working or personal relationships.

It's much more challenging to break these old patterns and establish new ones. So I suggest that you start with brief periods of time where you are giving your energy to someone you don't have any prior relationship with and you don't have any expectations from. For example, try it with the guy at the dry cleaners. The only thing you are expecting when you walk in there is that your clothes are ready for you. It's just a brief interchange—see if you can go in there and put all your attention on the person giving you your dry cleaning. Just stop a minute and ask, "How was your day?" and really listen to what he has to say.

I'm really good friends with my dry cleaner. I watch people rush in and rush out, drop off and pick up their clothes, with their attention completely on themselves and their day and where they need to be next. They give no attention to this guy who is putting a lot of time and love into making their clothes look good. So I make sure to give him my attention. He opens up; he's so happy to talk to me. And it changes how he is for the rest of the day. So I have an effect in a very small way—it's almost like a ripple in a pond. I have an effect on him, and then the next person coming into the shop sees him happier and smiling, and he has an effect on that person, and that energy travels out into the world.

You would be amazed how just giving a little attention to a stranger can allow that person to open to you. Try it with your cab driver, with the barista in your local Starbucks, with the UPS delivery guy. Try it in moments of stress and tension—like when a cop is giving you a ticket, when the printer hasn't printed your reports on time, when the passenger next to you on the train spills coffee on your leg, even when someone reverses into your car.

I do it every day when I arrive at work. I walk around to all the employees and I say good morning: I check in. I try to pick up on any problems, and if I see something I'll pull someone aside to ask if everything is okay and whether there is anything I can do. A lot of times it's not even a work problem, but a family problem. But the fact that they get to speak about it with someone who actually cares changes things for the rest of the day. The more people in the system are able to open up and flower, the healthier the system is. And the healthier the system is, the more people open up and have the room to be creative and loving.

Once you've practiced with strangers or work colleagues, and experienced for yourself what a powerful effect your attention has, you will want to try it with your spouse or partner, your children or your parents. Remember that it is infinitely harder in these types of relationships, because we expect so much from them that it's hard to stop coming to those relationships with a "taking" mentality.

When you feel ready to practice leaving that mentality aside, pick a specific time to begin. The best time I've found is when I walk through the door after work. Most people have made a conscious or unconscious decision to give their attention and energy at work because they understand the short-term benefit—to get paid. Then, by the time you get home, you are so burned out and depleted that you arrive with an expectation that your spouse will refill your attention and energy. And, of course, your spouse is quite likely feeling the same way—depleted and in need of attention—whether she has been out at work also, or at home taking care of the kids.

So, two people walk through the door at night, both expecting that the other person is going to give them attention and energy. They come to that meeting on the doorstep or in the kitchen with a taking mentality, and each meets a resistance in the other. Each person is trying to protect the little energy that they have left, and to take as much energy as possible from the other person. This is the cause of most of the tension that I see in relationships. Instead, I try to enter the house every evening with the thought that my wife needs my attention and energy and I'm going to give fifteen minutes of undivided attention and energy to her—just fifteen minutes of it before I fall back into taking mode and dump my problems and stress and negative energy into the relationship. Thankfully, what I've found is that after those fifteen minutes, most of my problems seem to dissolve, and the energy in the house stays positive.

It might be hard initially, especially when you're running low on energy, at the end of the workday, but if you come in with the idea that you are going to give as much of your energy and attention to the other person as possible, you'll find that when the other person is met with what he needs, he will be able to respond and give you more energy back. But it's very important that somebody is willing to break the dynamic of taking. And you have to do it unconditionally. It won't work if your motivation is simply to get the other person to do the same for you. It also won't work if you go home and explain this book to your spouse in the hopes that he'll change and start giving you more energy. I've seen people do that, but again, that's just a variation on the taking mentality. Ideally, both spouses consciously change the way they are operating and then there is much more energy in the household for everybody. But it always starts with you.

THE VIEW FROM THE TWENTY-FIFTH MILE

My favorite day of the year in New York City is the day of the marathon. The energy of the whole city is completely transformed for those few hours that the marathon is being run—partly because the runners are giving of themselves for a greater cause, but even more so, I think, because everyone else is so supportive of the runners.

I always go to the same spot, in the middle of Central Park, right at the end of the twenty-fifth mile. The runners come past there with just one mile to go. I head out when it's three or four hours into the race. Once I took my place in the crowd early, when the world-class runners were coming through, and it was totally unfulfilling. There was nothing they needed from me. But if you go three or four hours after the start time, when all the average Joes are conking out on that last hill, and you sit there and just cheer them on for an hour, I guarantee you, you'll be as high as a kite. *Come on! Keep moving! You can do it! You've almost made it!* (And of course, because it's New York, people will be yelling, *Get the f--- going! Move your ass! You have no f---ing option but to finish!*) Just from unconditionally giving these strangers your energy, you'll feel energized yourself. The marathoners are men and women just like you and me, of every shape and size, and you lift them up that last hill with your energy and support. It's an amazing thing.

Thanks to ING, who sponsor the marathon every year, I've been at the finish line and gotten to talk to the winners and a lot of people who finish the race early. And they have all told me that the energy they feel coming through that last mile, with everyone clapping and cheering and rooting for them, is overwhelming. What they are left with is not just the relief and euphoria of finishing the race, but the energy of all the people on the sidelines. I think that's why so many New Yorkers will say that the day of the marathon is the best day in New York. It's also one of the safest days in New York. Someone should do a study on the crime rate for marathon day compared to other days in the year—I'm sure it would be testimony to the power and potential that Expanding Your Awareness can have.

CHAPTER TWELVE

YOUR LEGACY

*This is the true joy in life, the being used for
a purpose recognized by yourself as a mighty
one; the being a force of nature instead of
a feverish selfish clod of ailments and
grievances complaining that the world will
not devote itself to making you happy. . . . I
want to be thoroughly used up when I die, for
the harder I work, the more I live. I rejoice in
life for its own sake. Life is no 'brief candle'
to me. It is sort of a splendid torch which I
have a hold of for the moment, and I want to
make it burn as brightly as possible before
handing it over to future generations.*

—*GEORGE BERNARD SHAW*

ONCE I FINISH THE PROCESS OF CREATING A CLIENT'S personal financial plan, helping them to save, earn, wisely invest, and contribute their money philanthropically, there is one final step we take. It is called estate planning, or legacy planning, and it is where the client decides what they want to happen with their money after they die. This is the point where the person has to stretch to think beyond their own lifetime and the benefits their money can bring them or even others they directly touch and ask, "What do I want my legacy to be? How do I want to be remembered? How do I want my impact to be felt when I am gone, by people who may not even know who I was?"

Now that we have reached this point in the book and gone through the four-step process of creating a "financial plan" for the new currency of attention, it is time to turn our focus to the question of our broader legacy. Let's take a moment to reflect on what we have learned, and then we can examine the question, What is the legacy of my attention and energy? What imprint will my expression leave on the world?

Through the first pillar, Connecting to Source, we learned how to save our attention, become conscious of how we are spending it, and spend it wisely. The practice of meditation helps us to break the illusory promise that something "out there" will give us the energy we crave, and instead connects us to an infinite source of energy that we can discover within our very own self.

Through the second pillar, Owning Your Unique Expression, we learned how to earn our energy—and our money—through doing what we love to do. Rather than seeking energy from outside ourselves, we discovered that by engaging our *unique creative expression* in the world, we can find a greater source of fulfillment. Because our creative expression or unique purpose generates energy as we engage in it, it gives more satisfaction than any object we could possess.

Through the third pillar, Redirecting Your Attention, we learned to invest our energy and attention in who we want to be in the future, freeing ourselves from constant preoccupation with trying to change the past and the present, and empowering us to build the life we dream of.

Through the fourth pillar, Expanding Your Attention, we learned the power of giving our energy and attention to others. We discovered what a tremendous gift we each have to contribute to the world through every interaction we have with another human being.

Now I want to take a moment to think about how this process translates into a meaningful legacy. The simplest way I ask clients to think about their legacy is to ask them, "How do you want to be remembered?" That immediately focuses them on tangible actions and contributions. I can't tell you how many times I've heard stories about someone who died wealthy but left no will or estate plan. The family will often say, "He used to talk all the time about what he wanted to happen after he died," but the sad truth is that because he never took action, most of that money ends up paying taxes or becoming the object of family squabbles. We don't remember people for the money they left sitting in a bank account—we remember them for what they contributed, what they supported, what they made possible.

IIII

We remember people for what they contributed, what they supported, what they made possible, not the money they left sitting in a bank account.

IIII

When it comes to our new currency, what you will be remembered for is what you give your attention to. And just as you have to make your estate plan while you are still alive, you have to start actively building the legacy of your attention right now. In fact, a legacy of energy and attention is not really about what happens after you die. Every action we take, every choice we make about where to put our attention and direct our flow of energy, creates ripples that can generate waves that can turn tides in this world. So there is a "legacy" to every moment.

I like the metaphor of a legacy because it encourages people to think completely beyond themselves, beyond any thought of getting something in return. It connects people to a much broader sphere of potential impact than their own circle of relationships. In the end, I believe the whole human race is one vast system, closely interrelated to the planetary system that supports life and is now also dependent upon us to support and sustain it.

What is interesting is that 200 years ago it would have been much harder to describe this notion to people without it seeming abstract. But today, in the age of the Internet, most of us are connected to a powerful metaphor for our interconnectedness on a daily basis.

The phrase "World Wide Web" literally conjures up an image to me of a spider web made up of six billion lines connecting all the people on the planet. During my lifetime, this amazing technology has emerged that can be seen as an outward manifestation of the idea that we are all one large system. Spiritual mystics have told us for millennia that we are all one, but now science and technology are starting to confirm that insight. In the early twentieth century, visionary Jesuit priest and paleontologist Pierre Teilhard de Chardin, author of *The Phenomenon of Man,* wrote about what he called the "noosphere," which he described as the "thinking layer" that surrounds our planet like an invisible envelope of collective human consciousness, in the same way that the biosphere encloses the planet in organic life. And some credit Teilhard with "predicting" the emergence of the Internet almost half a century before it was invented.

Albert Einstein, one of the greatest scientific minds ever to awaken on this planet, wrote:

> A human being is part of a whole, called by us the Universe, a part limited in time and space. He experiences himself, his thoughts and feelings, as something separated from the rest—a kind of optical delusion of his consciousness. This delusion is a kind of prison for us, restricting us to our personal desires and to affection for a few persons nearest us. Our task must be to free ourselves from this prison by widening our circles of compassion to embrace all living creatures and the whole of nature in its beauty.

To adapt Einstein's beautiful phrase, this book is about helping us to "widen our circles of attention." Maybe we all feel so alone and out of balance because we don't feel connected to a bigger whole. We all share the same doubts and fears, some of us just hide them better than others.

It helps in this process to know that you are not alone. I think that these days, more and more people are realizing this fact, and again, the Internet is playing a big part. Just a few years ago, someone with a particular niche interest or an unusual problem might have felt isolated, not knowing where to turn or who to talk to. But today, there are chat rooms on every conceivable subject, where like minds can connect and discover their sameness.

We all need connection, as human beings, and the broader our circles of connectedness, the more purposeful and meaningful our own life will become. As we widen our circles of attention, we simultaneously become aware of the impact that we can have, even if we are just one in six billion, one tiny node in the infinite web of humankind.

The broader our circles of connectedness, the more purposeful and meaningful our lives become.

Just as the Internet makes a great analogy for describing the interconnectedness of billions of people, it is also a great example of the potential impact of one ordinary individual. Have you ever heard of Vint Cerf? My guess is, probably not. I certainly hadn't until I happened to read about him in the back pages of *Esquire* magazine. But he impacts my life every day, because Cerf is the man credited with being the "father of the Internet." An American computer scientist, he developed the language that computers use to communicate over the Net (technically known as TCP/IP protocols.) What I find fascinating about Cerf (who insists that the fact that his name is pronounced "surf" is just a happy coincidence) is that he comes across as such an unassuming, ordinary man. Most people may not know his name, yet his invention touches the lives of billions of people every day. As he told *Esquire,* "there was no one 'Ah-ha!' moment"[1] where he saw what his idea would lead to. It was a process that unfolded over time. What I like about Cerf's example is that it points to the impact one individual can have—and the kind of legacy that can be created *within* a human lifetime, thanks to the miraculous speed of change.

Thinking about the legacy of your energy and attention requires stretching to see your connection to the broadest circle possible, and recognizing the importance of your own actions and choices in relationship to that greater whole. It's not necessarily about trying to take bigger actions to affect more people; it is about bringing the awareness of that larger context into every small action and interaction you have. And the most important thing to remember is that if you want to make a real difference, you have to start with yourself. You will be amazed at how actual sustained change in yourself can impact your corner of the world, and the legacy of your attention can keep expanding out into the wider world and forward into the future.

If this book has had an impact on you, I would urge you to be careful about how you try and share its message with others. Many of us have a tendency to take something new and pass it on to someone else. That's understandable—it's part of our human desire to share. But this actually has two negative effects. One is that unless you allow time to truly digest a work and practice it for yourself, you actually let yourself off the hook by passing it on. It's the mind's way of patting yourself on the back and telling yourself you've done a good job and now you don't have to practice.

Second, no one likes to be told anything unless they have asked for help first. Too often, someone I've coached will call me and say, "You know, what I learned from you yesterday really had an impact on me, but I went home and tried to *tell* my partner how to do it and she totally didn't get it. Maybe it's because I couldn't explain it well. Maybe if you could talk to her, you could help." But it never helps unless the other person genuinely wants help.

You're the one reading this book and you only have the power to change yourself. If you practice these techniques you will change, and people will see that change and come to you and ask what's going on. Then you have two choices—you can pass on your copy of this book, or you could share how your life has changed, while being careful not to tell your friends what they need to do or not do. Just as I ask you to be gentle with yourself, *be even more gentle with others.* They have their struggles, just like you, and if you really care you will listen first and share second. If this book has touched you, the way to share that is not to give other people advice, but to give them the precious currency that this book is all about: attention.

Once you stop trying to fix the people around you and instead focus on learning to listen and widening your circle of awareness as far as possible, what you will discover is that you will begin to have an impact in profound and unexpected ways. You will begin to leave a legacy for the future that is measured not in money, but in human energy that has been generated by your freely giving your attention to others. When you give your attention to another human being, that person suddenly feels met and fulfilled and will stop craving your time or stop endlessly taking. And when that man or woman goes home, his or her energy will be freed up to be given to others in turn. Freely given attention generates more energy, and energy fuels creativity. That's what your legacy to the world can be, in ways that you may not ever be able to see, but it will undeniably be felt by people far beyond the sphere of your personal relationships and by generations to come.

This book is part of my legacy—not for its original ideas or literary value, but because I've poured my attention and energy into it for the past two years, and I hope that through reading it, and giving it your attention for the hours it has taken you to reach these final pages, you will feel energized and inspired and begin to take action to transform your own life. If you do, then my legacy will live on through you and all those you give attention to, not as words and ideas, but as the kind of dynamic creative energy that is the only real happiness I know of. That's the kind of happiness that money can't buy, but attention, when freely given, can. And it really does have the power to change the world, one person at a time.

||||

Once you stop trying to fix people, you will begin to have an impact in profound and unexpected ways.

||||

My deepest personal and spiritual philosophy is that we do not need to seek outside of ourselves for completion, perfection, or fulfillment. We are already complete, as we are, and we are blessed with infinite potential. When you connect to Source and have the courage to forge your direction in life from a place of giving rather than taking, the laws of the universe will mysteriously begin to work in accordance with your wishes and dreams. There is nothing you need to get out there; but there is everything to give.

There is an infinite resource of energy within every human being that can be offered up to this world. Indeed, it is the world around us that is incomplete, that needs us to fulfill it and transform it and perfect it—and to sustain it with our infinite energy, passion, and creativity. The world is calling all of us. *Are you the one listening?*

NOTES

To be successful is to align our
individual strengths with the universal
source of energy to fulfill our deepest desires
in service to the world.

—*JEFFREY L. GITTERMAN*

CHAPTER 1

1. Michael Shermer, *The Mind of the Market* (New York: Times Books, Henry Holt, 2008), 149.
2. Daniel Gilbert, *Stumbling on Happiness* (New York: Vintage Books, 2007), xiii–xiv.
3. Gilbert, *Stumbling on Happiness*, xiv.
4. Lynne Twist, *The Soul of Money* (New York: W. W. Norton, 2006), 8.
5. Arthur Schopenhauer, *Religion: A Dialogue and Other Essays* (Manchester, NH: Ayer Publishing, 1973), 97.
6. Woody Allen, "Without Feathers," in *The Complete Prose of Woody Allen* (New York: Wings Books, 1992), 63.
7. Andrew Cohen, *The Promise of Perfection* (Lenox, MA: Moksha Press, 1998), 17–19.
8. Søren Kierkegaard, *Eighteen Upbuilding Discourses,* trans. Howard Vincent Hong (Princeton, NJ: Princeton University Press, 1990), 250.
9. Jason Zweig, *Your Money and Your Brain* (New York: Simon & Schuster, 2007), 231.
10. Zweig, *Your Money and Your Brain,* 41.
11. Essentials of Buddhism, Four Noble Truths, www.buddhaweb.org.
12. Sakyong Mipham, *Turning Your Mind into an Ally* (New York: Riverhead Books, 2003), 158.
13. Mihaly Csikszentmihalyi, *Good Business* (New York: Viking, 2003), 24.

CHAPTER 2

1. Max Planck, "Das Wesen der Materie" [The Nature of Matter], speech, Florence, Italy, 1944, Archiv zur Geschichte der Max-Planck-Gesellschaft, Abt. Va, Rep. 11 Planck, Nr. 1797.
2. H. A. Simon, "Designing Organizations for an Information-Rich World," in Martin Greenberger, *Computers, Communication, and the Public Interest* (Baltimore, MD: Johns Hopkins Press, 1971).
3. Thomas De Zengotita, *Mediated Glossary,* www.mediatedtdez.com/2005/03/mediated-glossary.html.
4. Ross Robertson, "The World I Built from Darkness: An interview with Zoltan Torey," *What Is Enlightenment?* 35 (January–March 2007), www.wie.org/j35/zoltan.asp.
5. John McCain, *Faith of My Fathers* (New York: Harper Perennial, 2000), 206–212.

CHAPTER 3

1. Mihaly Csikszentmihalyi, *Good Business* (New York: Viking, 2003), 188.

CHAPTER 5

1. Quoted in Thomas Egenes and Reddy Kumuda, *Eternal Stories from the Upanishads* (New Delhi: Smriti Books, 2002), 169.
2. Thich Nhat Hanh, *The Miracle of Mindfulness: A Manual on Meditation* (Boston, MA: Beacon Press, 1987), 20.
3. The Office of Tibet, official agency of His Holiness the Dalai Lama, London, http://www.tibet.com/Buddhism/om-mantra.html.
4. Rick Warren, *The Purpose Driven Life: What on Earth Am I Here For?* (Grand Rapids, MI: Zondervan, 2002), 89.
5. Sakyong Mipham, *Turning Your Mind into an Ally* (New York: Riverhead Books, 2003), 116.
6. Steven Levine, *A Gradual Awakening* (New York: Anchor Books, 1979), 29–31.
7. Andrew Cohen, *Evolutionary Enlightenment* (to be published 2009 by EnlightenNext).
8. Jack Kornfield, "A Mind Like Sky: Wise Attention Open Awareness," *Shambhala Sun* magazine, May 2003.

CHAPTER 6

1. Marcus Aurelius, *Meditations,* trans. Maxwell Staniforth (New York: Penguin Classics, 1964), 126.
2. Figures cited in "The Surprising Profit of Student Loans," *Fortune,* April 16, 2007.
3. Richard Branson, quoted in "Business 2.0: Branson's Next Big Bet," money.cnn.com/magazines/business2/business2_archive/2006/08/01/8382250/.
4. Daniel Kahneman *et al.,* "Would You Be Happier If You Were Richer? A Focusing Illusion," *Science 312,* 1908 (2006).
5. Bill Weir and Sylvia Johnson, "Denmark: The Happiest Place on Earth," *ABCNews.com,* January 8, 2007, http://abcnews.go.com/2020/story?id=4086092.
6. Lao Tsu, *Tao Te Ching,* trans. Stephen Mitchell (New York: Harper Perennial, 1992), ch.15.
7. Mihaly Csikszentmihalyi, *Flow: The Psychology of Optimal Experience* (New York: Harper Perennial, 1991), 4.
8. Elizabeth Debold, "Flow with Soul: An interview with Dr. Mihaly Csikszentmihalyi," *What Is Enlightenment?* 21 (Spring–Summer 2002).
9. Abraham Maslow, *The Farther Reaches of Human Nature* (New York: Viking Press, 1971).
10. Chip Conley, *Peak: How Great Companies Get Their Mojo from Maslow* (San Francisco: Jossey Bass, 2007), 14.
11. Abraham Maslow, *Motivation and Personality* (New York: HarperCollins, 1987).

CHAPTER 7

1. Eckhart Tolle, *A New Earth* (New York: Penguin, 2008), 258.
2. Steven Reiss, *Who Am I? The 16 Basic Desires That Motivate Our Action and Define Our Personalities* (New York: Tarcher/Putnam, 2000).
3. Abraham Maslow, *The Maslow Business Reader* (New York: Wiley, 2000), v.
4. Paul D. Zimmerman and Ruth Ross, "The New Jazz," *Newsweek,* December 12, 1966.

CHAPTER 8

1. Maslow, *The Farther Reaches of Human Nature.*

CHAPTER 9

1. Paul G. Thomas, *Advanced Psycho Cybernetics and Psychofeedback,* (Los Angeles: Paul G. Thomas/Psychofeedback Institute, 1982).
2. "The Technology of Universal Intelligence with Ray Kurzweil," interview in Melissa Hoffman, "Faster Forward: Impressions of Our Emerging Future," *What Is Enlightenment?* 23 (Spring–Summer 2003).

CHAPTER 10

1. Eckhart Tolle, *The Power of Now* (Novato, CA: New World Library, 1999), 1.
2. Tolle, *The Power of Now,* 2.

CHAPTER 11

1. Michael Schermer, *The Mind of the Market* (New York: Times Books, 2008).
2. Lynne Twist, *The Soul of Money* (New York: W. W. Norton), 45.
3. Twist, *The Soul of Money,* 74.
4. *New York Times,* "Make Money and Save the World," May 6, 2007.
5. Gary Hirshberg, "Why I Wrote My Book," *The Huffington Post,* comments posted on March 10, 2008, http://www.huffingtonpost.com/gary-hirshberg/why-i-wrote-my-book_b_90721.html.
6. All data in this paragraph from Patricia Aburdene, *Megatrends 2010* (Charlottesville, VA: Hampton Roads Publishing, 2005).
7. J. Krishnamurti, *This Light in Oneself: True Meditation* (Boston, MA: Shambhala Publications, 1999), 6.

CHAPTER 12

1. Cal Fussman, "What I've Learned: Vint Cerf," *Esquire,* May 2008.

RECOMMENDED READING

Books range in subject matter and readability so the author recommends previewing books before buying them to assure that you find the books that best suit your needs.

PILLAR 1:
CONNECTING TO SOURCE

The Power of Now by Eckhart Tolle

A Gradual Awakening by Stephen Levine

A Path with Heart by Jack Kornfield

Zen Mind, Beginner's Mind by Shunryu Suzuki Roshi

Embracing Heaven & Earth by Andrew Cohen

Freedom from the Known by J. Krishnamurti

Talks with Ramana Maharshi: On Realizing Abiding Peace and Happiness by Ramana Maharshi

The Miracle of Mindfulness: A Manual on Meditation by Thich Nhat Hanh

The Myth of Freedom and the Way of Meditation by Chogyam Trungpa

Tao Te Ching by Lao-tzu (any translation)

A Brief History of Time by Stephen Hawking

The Elegant Universe by Brian Greene

Turning Your Mind into an Ally by Sakyong Mipham

PILLAR 2:
OWNING YOUR UNIQUE EXPRESSION

The Laws of Lifetime Growth: Always Make Your Future Bigger Than Your Past by Dan Sullivan

A New Earth by Eckhart Tolle

Flow: The Psychology of Optimal Experiences by Dr. Mihaly Csikszentmihalyi

The Highest Goal: The Secret That Sustains You in Every Moment by Michael L. Ray

The Purpose Driven Life: What on Earth Am I Here For? by Rick Warren

Who am I? The 16 Basic Desires That Motivate Our Action and Define Our Personalities by Steven Reiss

PILLAR 3:
REDIRECTING YOUR ATTENTION

Advanced Psycho Cybernetics and Psychofeedback by Paul G. Thomas

Meditations: Creative Visualization and Mediation Exercises to Enrich Your Life by Shakti Gawain

You Can Heal Your Life by Louise Hay

PILLAR 4:
EXPANDING YOUR AWARENESS

The Seven Spiritual Laws of Success by Deepak Chopra

A Brief History of Everything by Ken Wilber

Giving: HowEach of Us Can Change the World by Bill Clinton

Living Enlightenment by Andrew Cohen

The Master Key System by Charles F. Haanel

Your Best Life Now by Joel Osteen

Minding Your Business by Horst M. Rechelbacher

Integral Consciousness and the Future of Evolution by Steve McIntosh

CONSCIOUS BUSINESS

Energy Leadership by Bruce D Schneider

The Soul of Money by Lynne Twist

The Seven Stages of Money Maturity by George Kinder

Conscious Business by Fred Kofman

Megatrends 2010: The Rise of Conscious Capitalism by Patricia Aburdene

Your Money and Your Brain by Jason Zweig

The Mind of the Market by Michael Shermer

The Fifth Disciple by Peter M. Senge

The New Retirementality by Mitch Anthony

INDEX

INDEX

INDEX